Branding Inside Out

Branding Inside Out

Internal branding in
theory and practice

Edited by Nicholas Ind

KoganPage

First published in Great Britain and the United States in 2017 by Kogan Page Limited

2nd Floor, 45 Gee Street	c/o Martin P Hill Consulting	4737/23 Ansari Road
London	122 W 27th Street	Daryaganj
EC1V 3RS	New York, NY 10001	New Delhi 110002
United Kingdom	USA	India

© Nicholas Ind 2017

The right of Nicholas Ind to be identified as the author of this work has been asserted by him in accordance with the Copyright, Designs and Patents Act 1988.

ISBN   978 0 7494 7890 2
E-ISBN   978 0 7494 7891 9

British Library Cataloguing-in-Publication Data

A CIP record for this book is available from the British Library.

Typeset by Integra Software Services, Pondicherry
Print production managed by Jellyfish
Printed and bound in Great Britain by CPI Group (UK) Ltd, Croydon CR0 4YY

CONTENTS

You can download resources for this book at
koganpage.com/BrandingInsideOut

ABOUT THE EDITOR

Nicholas Ind is an Associate Professor at Kristiania University College, Oslo and a partner in Equilibrium Consulting. Previously he ran Icon Medialab's brand consultancy arm in Sweden. Before he joined Icon, Nicholas had his own branding consultancy in the UK, was a director of a design group and was an account director in an advertising agency. Nicholas is the author of 12 books including *The Corporate Image, Terence Conran – The authorised biography, The Corporate Brand, Living the Brand, Brand Together* and *Brand Desire.*

Nicholas has a PhD from the European Graduate School in Switzerland. He is a former director of the Design Business Association (UK), a member of the advisory board of *Corporate Reputation Review* and the editorial board of the *Journal of Brand Management* and is Associate Editor of *European Business Review.* He is a Visiting Professor at ESADE, Barcelona and Edinburgh Napier University. He was a founder member of the Medinge Group, an international branding think tank.

ABOUT THE CONTRIBUTORS

Holger J Schmidt is a Full Professor of General Management and Marketing at Koblenz University of Applied Sciences, Germany, and Visiting Professor as well as guest lecturer at several academic institutions. He studied Business Administration in Mannheim and Barcelona and did his PhD in Hanover. His main subjects of research and teaching as well as consulting include brand management, brand orientation, internal branding, strategic management, technology marketing, empirical methods, social entrepreneurship and social businesses. Before his academic career, he held management positions in the consulting, advertising and logistics industries. Holger is the author of numerous books and academic publications, including the book *Internal Branding* which was, in 2007, one of the first of its kind.

Felicitas Morhart is a Full Professor of Marketing at the University of Lausanne (Switzerland). She graduated in Communication Science at the University of Munich and earned her PhD in Business Administration (2008) from the University of St Gallen (Switzerland). Her work lies at the intersection of marketing, positive leadership, and business ethics, such as her work on brand-specific transformational leadership, brand authenticity, and human branding. Her research has been published in the *Journal of Marketing, Journal of Consumer Psychology*, and *Management Accounting Research*, among others. Felicitas is a regular speaker at national and international academic and industry conferences. In addition, she develops and holds management seminars in the domains of cultural change and transformational leadership mainly in the automotive and finance industries. In 2013, she was named among the 'top 40 below 40' by the Swiss business magazine *Bilanz*.

Erika Uffindell is a Director of The Global Institute for Conscious Leadership. She founded Uffindell Group, a leading brand consultancy, and led the business for over 25 years. She is also a Partner in Pinea3 Living Organizations and a member of the Medinge Group. Erika has been advising leaders and organizations for over 25 years, inspiring them to embrace conscious business principles and build healthy and high-performing businesses. She is passionate about helping individuals and teams build greater levels of self-awareness to improve decision making, communication, relationships and trust. Her work is systemic, with a unique balance of the cognitive and experiential, and she has worked with global clients such as BNY Mellon, Ameriprise, Saks Fifth Avenue, RBS, HSBC, Columbia Threadneedle and Bond Dickinson.

Fathima Saleem is an Assistant Professor in the Department of Marketing Management at Ryerson University, Toronto. She completed her PhD at ESADE Business School in Barcelona. Fathima has a wide industry background ranging from brand consulting to digital media analytics, and has worked in the United Arab Emirates and Canada. In her current academic role, Fathima publishes collaborative research in the areas of online content creation and consumption, and brand-sponsored social media content. She has published in peer-reviewed journals on the topics of internal branding and consumer-brand relationships. She is also the recipient of numerous awards and research grants.

Oriol Iglesias is an Associate Professor at the Marketing Department and the Chair of the Research Group on Brand Management at ESADE Business School (Spain). Previously, at ESADE, he has also been Director of the Marketing Department, as well as Director of the ESADE Brand Institute. He is member of the Executive Committee of the European Academy of Marketing (EMAC). He is also member of the Editorial Board of the *Journal of Brand Management* and the Editorial Review Board of the *Journal of Product and Brand Management*. Oriol is the co-author of the book, *Brand Desire*.

Marije Scholma is Head of Internal and External Communications at NN Group. She is a communications professional with over 10 years of experience in a listed company, where she specialized in strategic communications and leading high-impact change programmes. She joined NN in 2005, and over the years has been responsible for the change communications in the merger of all the Netherlands-based insurance brands of ING into NN, the divestment from ING, and the IPO. Marije holds masters' degrees in Business Administration from the Radboud University, Nijmegen and in Corporate Communications from the Rotterdam School of Management.

Remco Barbier is Head of Branding at NN Group. He received his master's degree in Business Economics at the University of Tilburg. Remco started his career at ING Bank in 2004 as a marketing trainee. Over the years, he has managed ING Bank's mortgages campaigns, been manager of marketing for daily banking services, and led various marketing and communication change programmes. Before he joined NN Group he was part of the management team of ING Group's Sustainability department, responsible for marketing and communications.

Chris Kersbergen is Head of Employee Experience at NN Group. His background includes different marketing and communication roles within ING Group and agencies such as Euro RSCG and BBDO. After the global rebrand from ING to NN Group in 2015, Chris moved over from Branding to HR to help accelerate the transformation of the culture behind the NN brand. Chris holds a master's degree in Politics and Communication from the VU University Amsterdam, backed up by business courses at the Stanford School, Harvard, INSEAD and EURIB. He is co-author of a Dutch management book on Brand Culture.

Since 2010, **Carsten Baumgarth** has been Full Professor of Marketing and Brand Management at the Berlin School of Economics and Law. He has published more than 300 papers and books with a focus on brand management, B2B marketing, sustainable marketing, arts marketing and empirical methods. His work has been published in *Industrial Marketing Management, Journal of Business Research, European Journal of Marketing, Journal of Product & Brand Management* and *International Journal of Arts Management* among others. He has won more than 10 best paper awards. In 2012 he founded, together with colleagues, the Institute for Sustainability (http://institut-ina.de) in Berlin. Together with three colleagues he also founded the Expert Council for Technology Brands in 2015 (http://technologiemarken.de).

Lars Binckebanck is Full Professor of International Marketing at Furtwangen University (Germany). He has studied Management at the universities of Kiel (Germany) and Preston (UK), and his doctorate was obtained from the University of St Gallen (Switzerland). For more than 10 years, he has worked in practice as a market researcher, business consultant, sales trainer and, finally, managing director in the property development sector. He has authored and edited several books on sales management, and published more than 100 marketing-related papers.

Nick Pullan started his career in Investment Management for EY in London, before transitioning into HR, where he specialized in Resourcing and Employer Branding for financial, legal and non-profit organizations. This included five years with VSO, the international development charity, most recently as their Global Resourcing Manager and joint lead of the global People Brand project. Now Director of a fashion brand, which produces premium luggage and accessories, his focus is on building the company's presence in the UK and overseas markets. Nick is a Member of the Chartered Institute of Personnel and Development.

Hannah Gilman studied English and Modern Languages at Oxford University before joining Interbrand to work on brand valuation projects. She then worked at Citi as a Marketing Manager, where she was responsible for developing communications for different card brands. Following this, Hannah spent seven years at VSO as Brand and Communications Manager, where she had responsibility, alongside Nick Pullan, for the global People Brand project.

Rik Riezebos is Managing Director of EURIB (European Institute for Brand Management), located in Rotterdam, The Netherlands. He received his master's degree in Economic Psychology and followed the PhD programme in General Management at RSM/Erasmus University, Rotterdam. The title of his PhD thesis is *Brand-added Value; Theory* *and empirical research about the value of brands to consumers* (1994). Subsequently he was appointed (Associate) Professor at this faculty in the fields of Marketing Communication and Brand Management. In 2001, he founded EURIB, an institute that amongst other things organizes an accredited master's programme in Brand Management. In 2003, he published the text book *Brand Management: A theoretical and practical approach* and later co-authored the book *Positioning the Brand: An inside-out approach* (2012).

Steve Fogarty leads the Global Talent Futures team at adidas Group. Talent Futures drives innovation within the Global Talent Organization by leading the digitization of the talent experience, designing and building digital and analytics solutions, employer brand strategy and activation, and decision science. The team is responsible for trend spotting in the areas of digital, UX, social, design thinking, big data and analytics, decision science, and emerging areas of AI, VR and machine learning. The Talent Futures team spans the adidas Group globally and across brands and functions. Prior to adidas, Steve spent seven years at Waggener Edstrom Worldwide, where he developed and implemented integrated strategies to attract key talent. Steve served as a digital 'trend spotter' for the agency's staffing function as well as playing a key role in advancing the talent relationship capabilities with CRM and Web 2.0/social networking strategies. In his previous role at Waggener Edstrom he managed the recruitment function for the PR teams supporting key clients.

Christoph Burmann is a Professor at the University of Bremen in Germany and head of the Chair of Innovative Brand Management. He received his PhD from the University of Münster in Germany, where he studied Business Administration. He is editor of the book series *Innovative Brand Management* and author of brand management and marketing textbooks. Professor Burmann was guest lecturer at the Fudan University Shanghai and the SILC Business School at Shanghai University in China and the Judge Institute of Management Studies of the University of Cambridge in the UK. His research focus is in the fields of brand management, market-oriented management, strategic marketing as well as mobile marketing, consumer behaviour, and market research. He teaches undergraduate and postgraduate courses such as Marketing, Brand Management, Consumer Behaviour, and Marketing Research.

Rico Piehler is a post-doctoral researcher at the Chair of Innovative Brand Management at the University of Bremen in Germany. He received his PhD from the University of Bremen, where he studied Business Studies and Economics. He was a post-doctoral guest researcher at Griffith University in Australia and Temple University in the United States. His research in the area of internal and employer branding has been published in academic journals such as the *Journal of Brand Management* and the *European Journal of Marketing*. He teaches undergraduate and postgraduate courses such as Marketing, Brand Management, Consumer Behaviour, Marketing Research, and Applied Multivariate Data Analysis in Marketing.

The changing world of internal branding

01

NICHOLAS IND

In 1999 I attended the launch party for a new book on advertising and was asked by my publisher if I had any ideas for a new book. What about something like 'Living the Brand?' I suggested. It was an impulsive choice, but also reflected the work I had been doing over the previous three or four years in advising organizations on how to bring their brands to life. The book, which eventually came out in 2001 (with revised editions in 2004 and 2007), turned out to be quite influential. Reflecting back, I wonder why that was. I think there are three reasons. First, timing – while the dominant view of branding during the 1990s was led by a marketing communications perspective, the move towards services and the importance of experiences began to make managers realize that the way employees thought and behaved was increasingly important in creating a powerful brand image. While this transition was taking place in practice, there was virtually nothing written about the subject of what might be called integrated branding (the idea of unifying brand building around external communications and internal behaviour), nor internal branding. Second was a key case in the book – the outdoor clothing brand Patagonia. Having decided to write the book I was casting around for good examples. I remembered how, when I had been in the United States, I had visited a Patagonia store and how the staff had been highly knowledgeable and engaged. I contacted Patagonia and ended up spending a few days with them in California. The brand somehow encapsulated everything I wanted to say about Living the Brand, so I made the Patagonia story the opening chapter of the book. In subsequent years, I talked a great deal about the

Patagonia story in lectures and at conferences – it was a narrative that people truly engaged with. The third reason was the nature of the book, in that it combined theory and practice. At that time I was a consultant, but I was also doing some teaching in business schools. Consequently, I tried to combine an academic approach rooted in theory together with insightful cases, while bringing my experience of working with organizations to provide practical direction on how to bring a brand to life.

Since *Living the Brand* first appeared, the concept of engaging employees with a brand's vision and values has become more mainstream. The emergence of ideas around the persuasive concept of service-dominant logic, which suggests that everything is a service, has put renewed emphasis on how brands can create relevant experiences for their customers and other stakeholders (Vargo and Lusch, 2004; Grönroos, 2012; Grönroos and Voima, 2013). The development of co-creation has also put a focus on the greater opportunities for consumers and employees to engage directly with each other through the development of networks of mutual interest (Prahalad and Ramaswamy, 2003, 2004). I would argue therefore that the role of the employee in brand building has grown in significance, yet it has also changed. This is the heart of the matter that this book will address. Building on the themes of *Living the Brand*, *Branding Inside Out* draws on the innovative thinking of researchers and practitioners to show the evidence for an inside-out view of branding and to provide practical examples of how to do it. However, before summarizing the chapters you will find in this book, I first want to outline the key changes in the world of branding that are transforming the way we think about the relationships between organizations, employees and stakeholders; changes that provide a context for what you will read.

Loss of control

Loss of control sounds like a rather negative experience. If we lose self-control it induces a feeling of guilt and if we lose control of a situation it seems like we are at the mercy of decisions made by others.

Loss of control creates a feeling of anxiety, especially for managers brought up with the belief that their reason for being is precisely about control. Losing control over the brand is not inherently negative, however, but rather reflects the reality of the blurring of boundaries between inside and outside the organization, the growth of online brand communities and the speed of change in many industries. Most of all it reflects the fact that power has been ceded to customers and other external stakeholders (Kornberger, 2010). Managers still do, of course, have influence – strategies are defined by mostly senior people inside the organization; the products and services that are delivered to customers are still mostly designed inside the business (although open innovation practices are changing that); and the selection and presentation of what is offered are still mostly determined by internal expertise. Yet the familiar organization structures that many managers have grown up with are changing.

The typical control-based organization has a closed boundary – albeit informed by links to the outside world – where choices are made by managers and then implemented. This is a structured approach that may have relevance in an organization (or a part of an organization) where precision or repetition is vitally important, but it is generally predicated on a lack of trust in employees and a preference for control over spontaneity (Bauman 2001; Czarniawska, 2003). This type of organization assumes it has the ability to define its brand on its own terms. Its limitations are that it does not recognize the brand interactions that consumers have independent of the organization and it does not maximize the potential contribution of an organization's employees, who, given the opportunity, can contribute their ideas, their creativity, their knowledge and also access to their networks. It fails to recognize that employees can make significant contributions to the intellectual capital of the organization and can help to build the relationships that create brand desire (Ind and Iglesias 2016).

In place of the idea that the organization can control its brand is the counter idea that brands are largely organic. They are entities that emerge and develop in a space 'where multiple interactions occur and multiple conversations among different stakeholders take place' (Iglesias *et al.*, 2013). Employees, through the experiences they co-create, the conversations they have and the networks they take part in, are part of this process of organic brand creation. The neat linear pattern of an organization creating a brand and serving it to its customers and then generating feedback through market research has been replaced by something far messier and more polyphonic. Now we might learn about a brand as much through the blogs of employees, social media discussion and online fan communities as we do through official communications generated by the branding department. As an illustration of this, take a look at the Danish company, LEGO. It's a highly successful brand that has been built in recent times by its willingness to engage with people outside its corporate boundaries. LEGO's brand image is formed by marketing communications and co-branding activities, especially with film franchises such as *Star Wars*. Yet it is also built organically through the interactions consumers have with each other at the Brickfests they organize and the online fan communities they create through the LEGO Ambassadors programme and LEGO Ideas, where enthusiasts submit and then develop their product ideas together with LEGO. LEGO employees also interact with outsiders and involve them in creating innovations, such as the programmable LEGO Mindstorms NXT range that was designed by hackers, and the LEGO Architecture range that was prototyped by a fan. LEGO is a company that has shown the confidence to trust its employees, to let go of its brand and allow it to be developed through multiple voices. LEGO employees inspire and influence but they do not seek to control all the brand interfaces.

The key implication of this loss of control from the *Branding Inside Out* perspective is that the number of touchpoints between employees and external stakeholders is increasing in number and diversity. When someone for example is looking for a job they might visit a corporate LinkedIn page, check out a company's website and look at job boards, but they might also seek inspiration and contacts from their own personal and professional networks, look at online employee reviews and ratings and evaluate the experiences they have had as a consumer. To be judged positively, the organization has to recognize it cannot dictate exactly how employees should behave in all these contexts, and should rather work to create an environment that stimulates people to think for themselves and to respond to situations as they arise. As Felicitas Morhart argues in her chapter on leadership, citing the hotel chain Ritz Carlton, you need a culture of independent and creative thinking, where the organization 'transfers responsibility for the brand to each and every organizational member'. Forget the idea of controlling the way employees think and act and instead set them free to use their passion and skills in the service of the brand. This means that leaders need to be good listeners and good nurturers – able to stimulate engagement and provide support. Staffan Åkerblom, Head of Leadership and Organizational Development at Telia Company in Sweden, says: 'A company needs managers to function, but people do not necessarily need a manager. Instead they need to be empowered and to take responsibility for themselves.'

The new war for talent

In the 1990s, McKinsey undertook a year-long study of the world of work and coined the phrase 'The War for Talent'. The phrase described a globalizing world where people moved jobs more often, where the start-ups of the dot-com boom offered excitement and where intellectual capital was becoming a key source of competitive advantage. In this new war, there was a swing – at least for some – away from the corporation as the source of power, to the sought-after employee who could dictate their own terms. However, with the dot-com crash of 2000, this new world changed quickly and those sought-after employees often found themselves out of work. Now the war for talent is back and companies are having to work hard to make themselves desirable as places to work. Big technology companies such as IBM and Microsoft, consulting companies such as PwC and KPMG, and new start-ups are all competing for the same technology talent – for example network architects, user experience specialists and data analytics professionals. Indeed, in the 2015 Data & Analytics Global Study (commissioned by MIT Sloan Management Review and SAS) covering insights from 2,719 respondents, 43 per cent of the companies surveyed cited a lack of the appropriate data analytic skills as a key challenge (Ransbotham *et al.*, 2015). Referencing McKinsey Global Institute research, the study notes that it is estimated 'by 2018, the US economy will have a shortage of 140,000 to 190,000 people with analytical expertise and a shortfall of another 1.5 million managers and analysts with the skills to understand and make decisions.' In other words it is not only technologists that will be in short supply, but those around them who utilize technology. This tech shortfall is not easily addressed in the short term. Tech schools, such as the highly innovative École 42 based in Paris (with a branch in California), which has adopted a project-based approach using peer-to-peer learning which can take students anything from 18 months to five years to complete, has close to 5,000 attendees. It, and new tech schools like it, will provide the technologists that business needs, but for the foreseeable future the power will be with employees.

The consequence of the power shift is that companies will have to work hard not only to attract but also to retain their key people. One of the concepts that emerged alongside the war for talent in the 1990s was employer branding (Ambler and Barrow, 1996). This was the idea that while corporate branding espoused a focus on all stakeholders, the literature rather forgot about potential employees (Hatch and Schultz, 2003). Employer branding argued that an organization needed to think specifically about its offer to employees if it was going to attract the best talent. An evolution of employer branding was the concept of the Employee Value Proposition (EVP). Moroko and Uncles (2008) defined an EVP as a distinct package of benefits offered by the firm. They argued that an EVP must be unique, relevant and compelling if it was to act as a key driver of talent attraction, engagement and retention. This would seem sound but it is also potentially confusing, because, as Saleem and Iglesias (2016) have pointed out, the Corporate Brand, Internal Brand and Employer Brand all occupy similar territory. I would argue, based on their analysis of the literature alongside the experience of working for organizations, that there should only be one brand – the corporate brand. The corporate brand – if it is to have relevance – needs to be understood and supported by employees, which is the process of internal branding.

The rationale for internal branding is that if employees identify and engage with the brand they are better able to create relevant value for other stakeholders. As Christoph Burmann and Rico Piehler argue in Chapter 11 of this book: 'Successful brand management indirectly and directly depends on the delivery of the brand promise by employees.' By contrast, the process of employer branding is concerned with attracting and retaining employees (although some writers would argue it really only concerns the former). If there is an orientation in employer branding, it is dominantly human resources management, whereas internal branding (with its interest in the connectivity between employees and external stakeholders) uses the language of brand management more explicitly. So while the practices of internal branding and employer branding have different orientations they can comfortably co-exist when their respective roles are clear inside the organization.

Within this book there are examples of both internal branding – Marije Scholma, Remco Barbier and Chris Kersbergen's chapter on the international insurance business NN Group and Erika Uffindells's chapter on the law firm Bond Dickinson – and employer branding – Steve Fogarty on adidas and Nick Pullan and Hannah Gilman's story of the international charity VSO. The chapters illustrate the differences between employer branding and internal branding but they also point to where they fuse together in two specific ways. First, in the new war for talent, the organization must appeal to its core employee target markets in a compelling way. Yet spending time and money to attract new employees is not effective if the reality of the organization does not live up to what is communicated. The internal culture, style of leadership and ways of working can easily confound the claims made in recruiting campaigns. If employer branding has a specific orientation through its messaging towards attracting new employees, it is the way it combines with internal branding to build the organizational reality that helps ensure retention. Second, the departmentalized structure of organizations sometimes encourages managers to forget that potential employees not only see employer branding campaigns, they also read commentary on the business's environmental performance, experience buying the product or service, note the company's financial performance and hear through friends and colleagues about the company as an employer. The transparency of organizations means that companies need to be consistently good in all areas. This connectivity means different branding activities cannot be siloed. Rather they need to be integrated so that expectations and experience align for all stakeholders.

A consequence of the new war for talent is that sought-after employees become ever more demanding of employers. This might involve extrinsic rewards but it seems to be intrinsics that matter most. There is a belief that the organization must deliver on its side of the psychological contract and enable employees the flexibility to work in the way they think fit. It also means creating the conditions that enable people to grow and develop. For example, at sportswear brand adidas, there is a strong commitment to the development of mind and body. There are several reasons behind this. First is the location of the company's German head office in Herzogenaurach in Franconia – a small town far away from the hubs of European creativity such as Berlin, Paris, Amsterdam and London. Attracting and retaining designers, innovators and others is challenging. Second, the profile of the adidas work force is young and sports oriented (64 per cent are Generation Y) – they seek the opportunity to grow and to be active. Third is adidas's recognition of the importance of the intellectual capital of the organization and the need to enhance it by honing the knowledge and skills of its people. To fulfil its side of the bargain with its employees, adidas provides exceptional sporting facilities, but it also offers the possibility for continuous participatory learning with other learners, teachers, networkers and collaborators.

How people interact with purpose and values

One of the striking things about the Patagonia story that appeared in *Living the Brand* was how the Purpose of the organization (to use business to inspire and implement solutions to the environmental crisis) and its four values (Quality, Integrity, Environmentalism and Not Bound by Convention) were a lodestar for the way people behaved – something that Holger Schmidt emphasizes again in his chapter on brand-oriented cultures. Now the idea that a business should have a transformative, transcendental purpose that meets the needs of its different stakeholders and inspires individuals has become commonplace. However, as the Patagonia example illustrates so well, having the values is one thing; living them is another. Patagonia's employees use their Purpose and Values so comprehensively not because they have been inculcated with them through repetition, but because they align so well with the belief system of the individuals that work there. Patagonia adheres to its Purpose and promotes it to the outside world; not surprisingly, as a consequence, it tends to attract like-minded people. The advantage for Patagonia in this is that by creating a framework built on its Purpose and Values, it can empower its employees to deliver work on their own terms and to encourage people to innovate.

Two things to note about Patagonia's Purpose and Values are that they were defined through a participative process that looked back into the company's past and forward to the future, and they are simple to understand and use. They resonate with the individuals who work there, they are explained to employees and are used in decision making. Yet there is no demand from managers to live the brand. Engaging with the Purpose and Values is a choice that people make freely. This is different from pushing a brand at employees. Instead it recognizes that people are individuals who need to connect emotionally and intellectually with a brand on their own terms.

Similarly, the Swedish telecommunications business, Telia Company, has a corporate purpose and a set of values – Dare, Care, Simplify – which it communicates to employees, but the company argues that relying only on communication tends to make the ideas abstract. To develop employees into self-leaders and to generate the individual insight to bring the values to life, people now go through a workshop process that helps them to uncover and understand their own values. The argument is that by understanding oneself better, an alignment with the corporate values becomes something that an individual arrives at through discussion and reflection. As Frederic Laloux argues, organizations that encourage self-management and promote the opportunity for self-expression and creativity, aim to sense and respond, rather than predict and control. These organizations are more innovative and allow the workplace to 'become a place of personal fulfilment and growth' (Laloux, 2015).

This approach shifts the ideas of Purpose and Values away from a means of steering employee behaviour to a way of supporting the development of employees and their discovery of the meaning of the values in daily work. This shift is something Fathima Saleem and Oriol Iglesias note in their chapter as they quote Hatch and Schultz's neat aphorism that companies should 'stop asking how you can get your employees behind the brand and start thinking about how you can put the brand behind your employees' (Hatch and Schultz, 2008). One might think that this focus on the individual might diminish the importance of Purpose and Values, but it should make them more essential. When Purpose and Values are used as a means of control, the unity of the organization (much like in Hobbes's *Leviathan*) becomes the focus of activity. The question is then, 'how can we be more consistent as a brand?' And the answer resides in making people understand and use the brand. Yet, if the power of organizations is truly in its human capital, in the shared knowledge and skills of the individuals that comprise it, the perspective is wrong. We should forego this model in favour of one that emphasizes the people that comprise the organization (Foucault, 2003); in favour of welcoming heterogeneity (DeLanda, 2003) and the power of committed individuals working together. The question then becomes, 'how can we use the brand to support the creativity and inspiration of our people?'

Summary

The arguments above show how the thinking and practice of inside-out branding are changing. This book illuminates those arguments and others through the views of leading practitioners and researchers. In my experience these two areas do not interact enough. Academic researchers publish in academic journals, which rarely find their way onto the laptops or desks of practitioners, while practitioners perhaps rely overly on experience to make claims about the way things should be done without the evidence of research. Here you will find the research and models that prove the validity of internal branding as a process and also the examples that demonstrate how it works in practice.

References

Ambler, T and Barrow, S (1996) The employer brand, *Journal of Brand Management*, **4** (3) pp. 185–206

Bauman, Z (2001) *Community: Seeking safety in an insecure world*, Cambridge: Polity Press

Czarniawska, B (2003) Forbidden knowledge: Organization theory in times of transition, *Management Learning*, **34** (3) pp. 353–65

Delanda, M (2003) *A Thousand Years of Nonlinear History*, New York: Swerve

Foucault, M (2003) *Society Must Be Defended: Lectures at the Collége De France 1975–1976* (Éditions de Seuil/Gallimard, 1997). Trans. David Macey, New York: Picador

Grönroos, C (2012) Conceptualising value co-creation: A journey to the 1970s and back to the future, *Journal of Marketing Management*, **28** (13–14) pp. 1520–34

Grönroos, C and Voima, P (2013) Critical service logic: Making sense of value creation and co-creation, *Journal of the Academy of Marketing Science*, **41** (2) pp. 133–50

Hatch, M J and Schultz, M (2003) Bringing the corporation into corporate branding. *European Journal of Marketing*, **37** (7/8) pp. 1041–64

Hatch, M J and Schultz, M (2008) *Taking Brand Initiative: How companies can align strategy, culture, and identity through corporate branding*, San Francisco: Jossey-Bass

Iglesias, O, Ind, N and Alfaro, M (2013) The organic view of the brand: A brand value co-creation model, *Journal of Brand Management*, **20** (8) pp. 670–88

Ind N and Iglesias O (2016) *Brand Desire: How to create consumer involvement and inspiration*, London: Bloomsbury Business

Kornberger, M (2010) *Brand society: How brands transform management and lifestyle*, Cambridge: Cambridge University Press

Laloux, F (2015) The future of management is teal, *Strategy+Business*, 6 July

Moroko, L and Uncles, M D (2008) Characteristics of successful employer brands *Journal of Brand Management*, **16** (3) pp. 160–75

Prahalad, C K and Ramaswamy, V (2000) Co-opting customer competence, *Harvard Business Review*, **78** (1) pp. 79–90

Prahalad, C K and Ramaswamy, V (2003) The new frontier of experience innovation, *MIT Sloan Management Review*, **44** (4) pp. 12–18

Prahalad, C K and Ramaswamy, V (2004) Co-creation experiences: The next practice in value creation, *Journal of Interactive Marketing*, **18** (3) pp. 5–14

Ransbotham S, Kiron D and Prentice P K (2015) The talent dividend: Analytics talent is driving competitive advantage at data-oriented companies, *MIT Sloan Management Review*, April

Saleem, F Z and Iglesias, O (2016) Mapping the domain of the fragmented field of internal branding, *Journal of Product & Brand Management*, **25** (1) pp. 43–57

Vargo, S L and Lusch, R F (2004) Evolving to a new dominant logic for marketing, *Journal of Marketing*, **68** (1) pp. 1–17

Living brand orientation: how a brand-oriented culture supports employees to live the brand

02

HOLGER J SCHMIDT

The concept of brand orientation (BO) has been widely discussed in recent years. BO is described as a specific mindset that influences the brand-building process and brand-oriented behaviour of an organization and its members. Surprisingly, so far, BO has not been merged with learning theories to develop recommendations for the practice of internal branding. This chapter discusses the elements of a brand-oriented culture (values, norms, symbols), and shows how they can be connected with the brand behaviour funnel (I know, I can, I want) in order to encourage individual brand-oriented behaviour among employees.

Introduction

Brand management is a well-established field within and beyond the marketing discipline, and for decades, brand scholars have tried to identify and analyse the best ways to sustainably build and maintain successful brands. Traditionally, a lot of research has focused on ways to influence the perceptions of external stakeholders (customers, general public, and so on). More recently, employees have also come to be seen as a major target group for brand management. Reasons for the growing interest in this new discipline of internal branding are manifold: the increasing importance of the service sector and of services within other sectors; the more mature and critical consumer who does not believe in advertising and who expects a coherent brand experience; and the growing number of brand touch points which are, amongst other things, a result of the megatrends of digitalization (social media channels) and individualization. It seems logical that in a world where employees interact with customers in multiple ways, often beyond the control of the company, there must be more focus on the quality of these interactions. From a brand-oriented perspective, interactions must be inspired by the overall positioning of the brand.

Since the first internal brand management and internal branding publications appeared (for example, Keller, 1999; Thomson *et al.*, 1999), the question arose as to how employees can live the brand and, therefore, how companies can transfer their brand values and positioning to external stakeholders via employees' behaviour (see Saleem and Iglesias, 2016 for an overview). Much of the research in this field has focused on instruments that should lead to brand commitment and employees' brand-related behaviour. In a behaviouristic tradition, researchers have attempted to identify the 'hot buttons' that can transform established employee behaviour (for example, being friendly) into behaviour that would strengthen the brand and express its values, namely brand-driven, brand-related or brand-oriented behaviour. The general advice that has been given to practitioners includes to manage carefully their internal communication activities, to consider brand management within the field of human resource management, and to encourage a more transformational leadership style among their managers (Burmann *et al.*, 2009b; Du Preez and Bendixen, 2015; Mahnert and Torres, 2007; Morhart *et al.*, 2009). More specifically, measures like publishing a brand handbook for internal audiences, printing brand values on T-shirts and other internal giveaways, organizing events to celebrate the brand, chatting with the CEO in an internal blog about brand-related topics, training new staff about the brand, aligning pay systems with the brand values, and generally being more inspiring to staff members, were among some of the proposals. It is undisputable that those insights were highly relevant and quickly gained acceptance in practice. However, it must also be said that background factors that could positively stimulate employees' brand-related behaviour, such as the culture of a company or its organizational structure, were less often considered (an exception is Burmann and Zeplin, 2005).

This myopia of research in the field of internal branding is even more worrying today, when the discipline of brand management is in transition (Ind, 2014). With the new paradigm of co-created brands, the brand can no longer be seen as the result of activities of the brand's management only, which include the definition of an authentic, differentiating and relevant brand identity, the correspond-ing positioning and the implementation of the brand's values through integrated marketing communications and other brand-related activ-ities (Ind *et al.*, 2013). Within the predominant and so-called organic or agile logic, brands are the result of activities that are initiated by both the company and its stakeholders (Iglesias *et al.*, 2013). Both contribute to the meaning of the brand, the first one via owned and paid media, and the latter ones via word of mouth, posts, reposts, shares and reviews, amongst others, which contribute to a brand's earned media and offline reputation. If this is true, how can employ-ees contribute to overall brand strength by aligning their behaviour with a brand's positioning and values? If what we call a brand is the result of a permanently ongoing bilateral negotiation between a brand's management and its stakeholders, and if brand value is more and more created through conversations between employees and external target groups, the question arises whether the button to push in order to influence employees' brand-related behaviour exists at all (Saleem and Iglesias, 2016, p. 43). Maybe, as Henkel *et al.* (2007, p. 310) propose, managers should focus on the creation of an organizational environment 'that enables employees to find their own individual ways of articulating a brand to customers'.

Considering these arguments, it seems more important to establish a brand-driven culture that supports employees to take the right decisions and to show appropriate brand-related behaviour. Surprisingly, within this context, the concept of brand orientation has received little attention so far (Baumgarth, 2010). It goes without saying that within such a culture, the brand is considered to be one of the most important assets and, therefore, its elements could serve as a point of reference for all activities within the organization. Building on this, the question remains how a brand-oriented culture can be implemented. The forthcoming sections aim to provide answers in this regard.

Brand orientation, learning theories and a corresponding framework

The concept of brand orientation

Strategic orientations have been defined as guidelines that, implicitly or explicitly, influence the specific culture and behaviour of a company (Noble *et al.*, 2002). Market orientation, entrepreneurship orientation and technology orientation, as well as brand orientation, are prominent examples of strategic orientations (Schmidt *et al.*, 2015), but while the first three have been discussed for decades, the latter concept was introduced into literature only about two decades ago (Urde, 1994, 1999). The basic idea of brand orientation is that brands are important strategic assets of a company. Therefore, brand orientation focuses on the creation and nurturing of strong brands. Brand-oriented companies emphasize the importance of well-defined brand identities and centre around activities such as brand-related marketing communications and market research about the brand. Overall, and considering different settings and industries, there is plenty of evidence that suggests that a high degree of brand orientation positively affects the market and the economic success of companies (for example, Baumgarth, 2010; Yin Wong and Merrilees, 2008; Napoli, 2006; Bridson and Evans, 2004).

Building on the seminal model of corporate culture, as suggested by Schein (2006) and adapted by Homburg and Pflesser (2000) to the market orientation context, Baumgarth (2010, 2009) and Urde *et al.* (2013) propose a model of brand orientation which has been elaborated upon in more detail by Schmidt and Baumgarth (2014). Their model includes two layers: the first layer is called brand-oriented culture and includes values, norms and symbols of brand orientation. Values are defined as deeply embedded, taken-for-granted, and largely unconscious behaviours. They form the core of culture and determine what people think should be done. Norms, namely conscious strategies, goals and philosophies, represent the explicit and implicit rules of behaviour. In an organization, they determine how the members represent the organization, both to themselves and to others. Symbols and artefacts are the most explicit element of culture. They include any tangible, overt or verbally identifiable element in an organization (for example, furniture, dress code, stories, and jokes). The second layer is called brand-oriented behaviour, which includes behaviours that involve analysis (for example, brand research, brand controlling and measurement of brand equity) and other brand-related activities (for example, decisions about the marketing mix). The authors suggest that a brand-oriented culture drives a brand-oriented behaviour, but they also consider that there could be a flow-back from behaviour to culture. Figure 2.1 illustrates the corresponding model.

Building on this, a brand-oriented culture is an antecedent of employees' brand-related behaviour. Applying the concept to the Patagonia case that Ind (2007) analyses in his ground-breaking book *Living the Brand* helps to understand its full potential. Patagonia, an outdoor clothing company based in Ventura, California, is an organization with a strong and meaningful brand and a distinctive culture. Some of the most impressive elements of their culture can be assigned

Figure 2.1 Model of brand orientation (Schmidt and Baumgarth, 2014)

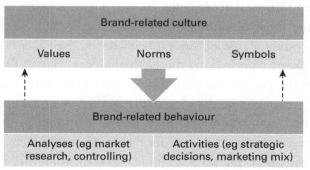

to the different layers of the brand orientation model, as explained in the following paragraphs, which contain, unless indicated otherwise, information from the work of Ind (2007, pp. 3–13).

Values

The young Yvon Chouinard, founder of Patagonia and a passionate climber, started a business producing climbing pitons. The quality of those pitons was of utmost importance, because inferior pitons could endanger the climber's life. It is not surprising that an obsession for quality can still be observed in Patagonia's business activities today. Some years later, Chouinard realized the environmental damage the pitons caused on well-trodden climbing routes. Notwithstanding the potential losses, he immediately pulled out of the piton business and began to offer aluminium chocks, which could be wedged in by hand, but which were almost unknown in the United States. Obviously, a strong environmental concern is still part of Patagonia's business model, and this comes to life when the company advises its employees how to abseil from buildings and then to reveal protest banners containing environmental messages. In a nutshell, there is strong evidence that the brand's values, among them 'quality' and 'environmentalism', are embedded in the company's culture and unconsciously drive employees' behaviours.

Norms

Though the management of Patagonia did not write down rules of behaviour for their employees, the company has clearly defined norms that should assist managers to take the right brand-related decisions and to support staff to live the brand. Their mission statement is perhaps the most obvious norm (Patagonia, 2016), namely: 'Build the best product, cause no unnecessary harm, use business to inspire and implement solutions to the environmental crisis.' Other norms are set by the explicit formulation of four core values of 'quality', 'integrity' 'environmentalism' and 'not bound by convention', which were defined and articulated by a cross-functional group of some 30 employees. As a result, outdoor enthusiasts and environmental activists enjoy working for Patagonia – and by voluntary choosing to follow the norms, they contribute to the living of the brand.

Symbols

At Patagonia, many brand-related symbols can be observed. The 28-page book, *Defining Quality*, describes the company's understanding of quality and therefore offers explicit norms – but the book itself is a clear sign that the corresponding brand value is of paramount importance. The surf report displayed daily on the board in the entrance hall of Patagonia's main office in Ventura, which is based on insider information, shows how deeply connected the company is with its customer base. The fact that visitors are asked to serve themselves in the staff canteen when they arrive early for a meeting is another sign of integrity and transparency. That employees are encouraged by management to leave work and to head to the beach when the waves are ideal for surfing, is a sign of the strong bonds that connect the company with its origin.

Behaviour

In the case study, Chip, Patagonia's receptionist at Ventura, states: 'I'm genuinely feeling groovy. It's seamless for me to give customer service and interact with people and to give them that feeling that it is a different place; that it is a business where you can be yourself.' Later, Chip continues: 'The best bit is… being the image and voice of Patagonia. I think my job is one of the most important in the company.' Obviously, Chip acts in a brand-related manner and therefore helps to bring the spirit of the Patagonia brand to life. We do not know how much of his behaviour can be attributed to the values, norms and symbols. But there is strong reason to believe that, overall, Patagonia's brand-oriented culture has had tremendous influence on him – and one can assume that the same applies to other staff members too.

To sum up, the concept of brand orientation can help to better understand which factors would support employees to live the brand. Nevertheless, so far it remains unclear how a brand-oriented culture can be implemented. Does its strength mainly depend on a founder's inspiring vision and his beliefs on how things should be done, as may seem to be true for Yvon Chouinard and Patagonia? Or can a company intentionally implement a brand-oriented culture and teach its employees about it? And, if yes, how can this be done? In order to find answers to these questions, it is useful to consider relevant insights from psychology about the broad field of learning.

Learning theories and the brand behaviour funnel

The field of organizational learning has been discussed for decades (Cyert and March, 1963). Though the idea of double-loop learning, which concentrates on learning from failure, has gained a lot of popularity (Argyris, 1991, 1999, 2005), a commonly accepted theory of the learning organization does not yet exist and therefore discussions around that topic are often linked to individual learning, where a broad range of well-studied theories and a long body of corresponding literature prevail (Rosenstiel, 2003, p. 460). Basically, learning theories suggest that learning can take place in at least four ways (Schuler and Moser, 2014, pp. 144–145). *Behaviourists* claim that learning results in a change of behaviour, which can, amongst other things, be attributed to the learner's reaction to certain stimuli (for example, classic or emotional conditioning). *Cognitive theories* interpret learning as a result of the acquisition of knowledge. This implies, *inter alia*, that repetition is needed to consolidate new information and to relate it to existing knowledge. *Constructivism* acknowledges that knowledge is not only based on the availability of information, but also on the individual's abilities to obtain and use relevant evidence. *Information processing theories* focus on mental processes and analyse how people store information, relate it to existing knowledge, and retrieve it from memory when needed (Schunk, 2012, p. 164). Commonly, it is accepted that *motivation* mediates the learning process: for example, the elaboration likelihood model suggests that people in high-involvement situations will be more likely to learn sustainably and, as a result, to change their attitudes, than others in low-involvement situations (Petty and Cacioppo, 1986). It is also obvious that without motivation, competences will not be transformed to goal-oriented action (Brandstätter and Schnelle, 2007, p. 51). In line with this, Schuler and Moser (2014, p. 491) argue that 'not knowing', 'not being able to' and 'not wanting' are among the main reasons why change processes fail.

Drawing on the aforementioned, personal behaviour (*I act*) can be explained as a function of personal knowledge (*I know*), skills and resources (*I can*) and motivation (*I want*) (Vroom, 1964; Campbell and Pritchard, 1976; Rosenstiel, 2003, p. 224). Wentzel *et al.* (2014)

transfer those insights to the field of internal branding and suggest a framework, which they call the brand behaviour funnel. They argue that employees must first know and understand what the brand stands for and how their behaviour impacts the brand-building process. Second, employees should be committed to the brand. Third, they need to possess the skills and tangible resources to translate the brand's values when interacting with customers. Only when those three components align can staff behave in a way that supports the brand.

Reflecting on the brand behaviour funnel may help to explain why some brand management initiatives fail. Obviously, it is not enough to print posters, or to design giveaways with the brand logo and an effective slogan which express the brand's ideology: employees must know what kind of behaviour is 'on brand'. At first glance this might seem evident, but it is not in most cases. This is an issue of both skills and resources. It may be difficult for a salesperson, for example, to express abstract values such as passion, performance or innovation. Perhaps the salesperson knows what the brand stands for and has been told how they should behave in the showroom in order to be on-brand, but does their personality allow them to greet every new prospect enthusiastically as a means to express the brand value 'passion'? Can they still deliver 'performance' after eight hours of hard work? Do they have access to the necessary resources (for example, equipment or electronic systems) to express the brand value 'innovation'? Can they display the kind of behaviour that supports the brand's values? The brand behaviour funnel suggests why even committed staff might not show brand-related behaviour: they may lack brand knowledge or brand-related skills and resources.

Introducing the Living Brand Orientation framework

Brand-related behaviour can only occur when a company's approach to internal brand management is embedded within a supportive culture (Saleem and Iglesias, 2016, p. 50). Employees need to know, like and use the brand's values, norms and symbols and have the skills and resources to act in a brand-supportive manner. To better understand how companies can use the insights of brand orientation research and learning theories for the sake of a better alignment between their employees and the brands, the following three case studies are testimony to successful brand implementation: TNT Express, Burberry and Paperproducts Design.

CASE STUDY TNT Express

Surprisingly, in 2007, the German subsidiary of the global logistics company **TNT Express** topped an industry survey of the strongest brands in the German parcel market. At the same time, the company achieved one of its best financial results ever. This was even more remarkable since Germany was not the home market of TNT (DHL, with its global headquarters in Bonn, Germany, had a huge market share) and in earlier rankings the company had been an also-ran. What had happened? Management attributed the new status as an admired brand partly to a branding project that started in 2003. In September of that year, the company specified project goals, established a steering committee and set a plan. In the following months, over 1,400 customers, employees from all levels and departments, as well as drivers, were asked to state their opinion about the TNT brand. This was partly done via telephone and personal interviews and partly by way of workshops. In the next project phase, which was termed 'defining the brand identity', the executive team analysed the results of the research and, in an attempt to include a more co-created view, extended the discussions to senior and middle management, functional groups (for example, apprentices) and external partners, and worked on a brand book. The analysis helped to develop a common understanding of what the brand was all about and consequently the brand ideology was defined and written down. In the next step, 300 employees were asked to comment on the new value proposition in workshops and to provide proposals for brand-related projects. The idea of those projects was to define ways to bring the brand's core and its values to life. More than 40 long-term projects and immediate measures were identified. Accordingly, the executive team decided to establish a programme management plan to install project groups and to implement the proposals. The results of the projects were regularly monitored in board meetings. Parallel to the implementation process, an internal communication campaign was elaborated and executed, involving many different communication channels. Some months after the kick-off of the internal campaign, an external campaign was launched to reach out to actual and potential customers. In the following years, market research about the brand was intensified, and the brand became a permanent area of consideration. The brand-oriented approach of the German TNT subsidiary lost speed in 2009 when, also as a result of the financial crisis, more and more decision structures were centralized within the corporate group, and came to an end when rumours began to circulate that TNT Express would merge with UPS. Today, following the involvement of the European cartel authorities, TNT Express is part of Federal Express.

The case has been well described from a practitioner's perspective (Seifert and Schmidt, 2006; Kraus *et al.*, 2007). From the viewpoint of brand orientation, and also considering the brand behaviour funnel discussed in this paper, the following facts, amongst others, seem of major interest. First, the executive team openly supported the project. Second, the brand ideology was communicated intensively, initially internally and then externally. Third, the brand values were defined in a unique way, and as a result employees strongly identified with the brand. Fourth, many norms of brand-oriented behaviour were set in place: the brand book described typical brand-related actions, and a guide for a brand-centric approach to leadership was published, based on the discussions of two groups of senior managers. Fifth, employees and drivers, with the support of the company's academy, were trained to follow the rules. Sixth, symbols of brand management played a crucial role: giveaways and communication materials that displayed the branding model were produced and distributed. The company's newsletter featured specials about the brand and explained brand-related topics. Senior managers permanently had to carry a personal identifier with them, and this included the main rules for a brand-oriented leadership culture. Seventh, the company's CEO regularly visited the welcome training of new employees to talk about the brand. Games, quizzes, competitions and sweepstakes were implemented, which all centred on the idea of living the brand's values. Last, but not least, the headquarters' entrance hall was redesigned to represent brand positioning in a more prominent way.

CASE STUDY Burberry

A second case that received international attention is that of the luxury fashion brand **Burberry**. The brand is successful at present, but in the early 2000s it faced serious problems. In an article in the *Harvard Business Review* (Ahrendts, 2013), former CEO Angela Ahrendts explains how she turned around the failing brand through a courageous restructuring process. It was interesting how she and her chief designer Christopher Bailey concentrated on a modern and innovative interpretation of the values of Burberry, which could be described as craftsmanship and Britishness (Phan *et al.*, 2011, p. 217). During the transformation of the company, Ahrendts relied on strict norms to strengthen brand implementation. One of the norms, in contrast to the previously decentralized approach, was that Christopher Bailey had to check and approve every new product that the customer would see. It was his job to make sure that the design was identifiable as a true piece of Burberry. The iconic trench coat was the symbol of the new focus on the corporate heritage of the brand. The product was a typical British product, but in spite of its aura it wasn't being sold at a premium price. Ahrendts raised the prices of the coat, initiated new innovative designs and made sure that the trench coat was always visible on the first page of Burberry's website. Additionally, the transformation of the brand was supported by intense sales and service initiatives. From a learning perspective, more emphasis was placed on staff product training and the stores were equipped with iPads and screens to visualize and accentuate the new approach, not only to clients but also to service personnel. Furthermore, a new pay scheme was developed to support staff's motivation to sell higher-priced products such as the trench coat.

CASE STUDY Paperproducts Design

The company **Paperproducts Design** (PPD), based in Germany, is one of the world's market leaders in designer paper towels. With about 130 employees and many independent sales representatives located in different countries, PPD produces around 15 billion packages of paper towels a year, accounting for about €20 billion of revenue. But how did a small company like this make it to US talk show queen Oprah Winfrey's list of favourite things for Christmas 2015? The company's management is convinced that part of the credit must be attributed to their brand: they firmly believe that their brand is not about paper towels but about being creative. Therefore, on the one hand, they organize their business around the idea of being a fashion company by creating two main lines during the year (spring/summer and fall/winter), employing trend scouts, exhibiting at design fairs and working together with internationally known designers. Conversely, they involve employees and customers at different stages in their design processes, and extended their product offerings to various items around the set table such as coffee mugs, plates and placemats.

In 2014 PPD invested in brand research: customers and employees were interviewed about their perceptions of the brand. The results were discussed in a project group, which included people across all departments and from different levels. This process led to the definition of a renewed brand ideology, including a sharpened positioning and value proposition. After completion of this step, one of the first measures of the management was to present and discuss the new approach with all employees in a one-day event at the company's headquarters. The brand ideology was summarized in a huge poster, which was placed on the staircase of the main building, and was hence visible to everybody who passed by the entrance hall and wanted to visit the administrative offices. Subsequently, sales representatives from all over the world attended training at the headquarters, while projects were established to improve brand-related performances in many areas, such as the internal design process. Additionally, the founder of the company participated in industry meetings and brand management conferences to talk about the brand.

What do the above three case studies have in common? TNT, as well as Burberry and PPD, defined values, set up norms and used symbols to implement their brand internally. And they were, implicitly or explicitly, aware of the brand behaviour funnel and used a broad range, or at least some instruments, to make sure that employees knew what the brand stood for, and could, therefore, act according to the brand's values whilst behaving in a manner that encouraged a positive brand experience for others. For example, TNT used workshops and an internal communication campaign to discuss the values of the brand and to make the norms known to their internal audience. They trained their people to adhere to the rules, implemented recruiting guidelines to select people that would fit the brand and used diverse brand-related symbols, which were popular amongst staff. At Burberry, sales assistants could learn about the long heritage of Burberry and its trench coat via movies, and the new pay scheme encouraged people to act in a brand-related way. At PPD, employees were introduced to the sharpened brand ideology in a one-day event in which they actively participated so that they could emotionally connect with the brand. They also observed the company's founder talking about the importance of the brand, which helped them to understand what kind of behaviour was expected of them.

As a result of the theoretical concepts that were introduced earlier in the chapter and the discussion of the case studies above, a framework was developed which explains how brand orientation can be systematically built and spread throughout a company. The Living Brand Orientation Framework (LBO-F) is displayed below in Figure 2.2.

The framework defines some preconditions that should be established if values, norms and symbols are to be implemented with the help of the brand behaviour funnel. Those preconditions include the existence of a brand ideology in terms of a brand's vision, mission, goals, and, most important, values (Saleem and Iglesias, 2016, p. 48). Ideally, the brand ideology should be developed in a co-creative manner by management and employees together, and since other (external) stakeholders such as customers and brand partners continuously add meaning to the ideology, it should be permanently updated. Accordingly, norms that are defined as conscious brand-related rules as well as brand-specific symbols should be established.

The framework suggests that brand-related behaviour is more likely to emerge if the elements of a brand-oriented culture are conciliated by means of the brand behaviour funnel. It is insufficient to define brand values, to put brand-related norms into place and to create symbols of brand orientation. What is often considered to be the goal of a brand management project is just its launching pad. Without values, norms and symbols, brand management projects are likely to fail – but their existence does not guarantee the creation of

Figure 2.2 The living brand orientation framework (LBO-F)

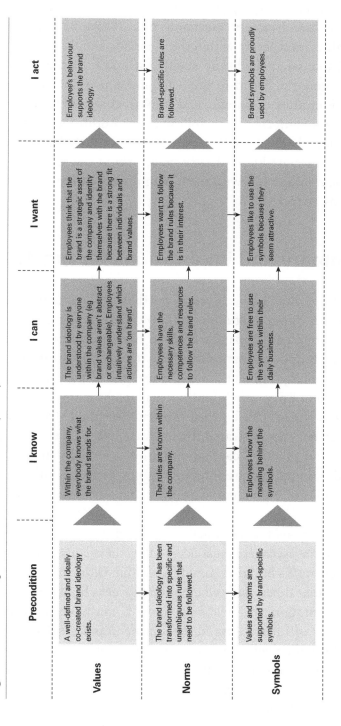

	Precondition	I know	I can	I want	I act
Values	A well-defined and ideally co-created brand ideology exists.	Within the company, everybody knows what the brand stands for.	The brand ideology is understood by everyone within the company (eg brand values aren't abstract or exchangeable. Employees intuitively understand which actions are 'on brand'.	Employees think that the brand is a strategic asset of the company and identity themselves with the brand because there is a strong fit between individuals and brand values.	Employee's behaviour supports the brand ideology.
Norms	The brand ideology has been transformed into specific and unambiguous rules that need to be followed.	The rules are known within the company.	Employees have the necessary skills, competences and resources to follow the brand rules.	Employees want to follow the brand rules because it is in their interest.	Brand-specific rules are followed.
Symbols	Values and norms are supported by brand-specific symbols.	Employees know the meaning behind the symbols.	Employees are free to use the symbols within their daily business.	Employees like to use the symbols because they seem attractive.	Brand symbols are proudly used by employees.

employee brand equity (King and Grace, 2010) and, correspondingly, external brand success (Burmann *et al.*, 2009a; Baumgarth, 2010). As for values, everybody within the company should identify with them and know what the brand stands for and how they can contribute to bringing the brand to life. Unambiguous rules of brand-oriented behaviour must be known, and employees should have the resources, skills and competences to follow them. Additionally, sticking to the rules must be in the self-interest of the staff. Reflecting on symbols, employees must know the meaning behind them, should be able to use them or connect with them within their daily work, and perceive them as attractive.

Summary and implications for practice

Brand orientation is a concept that has recently been widely discussed. Several studies within different industries show that brand-oriented companies seem to be more successful than others. Though brand orientation has been defined as a strategic orientation that implicitly influences the culture and behaviour of a company and its employees, the question remains how the knowledge of this research stream can be used explicitly to build strong brands. This chapter has demonstrated, through the use of a theoretical presentation and practical case studies, how a model that breaks down a brand-oriented culture into values, norms and symbols and applies basic rules of individual learning, can contribute to development in this field.

Implications for the practice of brand management are manifold: first, brand managers must accept that they can set basic parameters for their staff's brand-oriented behaviour. Ultimately, though, it is the culture that determines whether employees choose to support brand implementation via their behaviour: a causal relationship between measures of internal brand management and results in the form of brand-oriented behaviour may exist in theory, but cannot be assumed in practice. This also implies that brand managers need to accept a biased situation: even if it is not wise to set any rules, rules that are too strict and explicit about brand-related behaviour will not be helpful. Second, brand management should explicitly look at how the brand's values, norms and symbols can be implemented in a way that employees become aware of them, understand them, are able to apply and use them, and also like them. Last, but not least, internal brand management can only be as good as brand management itself. If the preconditions are not set in the right way, namely if there is no clear view on the brand ideology and the corresponding norms, and if no brand-related symbols have been identified and introduced, internal brand management is not likely to be successful.

References

Ahrendts, A (2013) Burberry's CEO on turning an aging British icon into a global luxury brand, *Harvard Business Review*, **91** (1), pp. 39–42

Argyris, C (1991) Teaching smart people how to learn, *Harvard Business Review*, **69** (3), pp. 99–109

Argyris, C (1999) *On Organizational Learning*, Oxford: Blackwell Business

Argyris, C (2005) Double-loop learning in organizations: A theory of action perspective, in Smith, K G and Hitt, M A (eds.) *Great Minds in Management: The process of theory development*, Oxford University Press, pp. 261–279

Baumgarth, C (2009) Brand orientation of museums: Model and empirical results, *International Journal of Arts Management*, **11** (3), pp. 30–45

Baumgarth, C (2010) 'Living the brand'. Brand orientation in the business-to-business sector, *European Journal of Marketing*, **44** (5), pp. 653–71

Brandstätter, V and Schnelle, J (2007) Motivationstheorien (Motivation Theories), in Schuler, H and Sonntag, K (eds.), *Handbuch der Arbeits- und Organisationspsychologie (Handbook of Industrial and Organisational Psychology)*, Hogrefe, Göttingen, pp. 51–65

Bridson, K and Evans, J (2004) The secret to a fashion advantage is brand orientation, *International Journal of Retail & Distribution Management*, **32** (8), pp. 403–11

Burmann, C, Jost-Benz, M and Riley, N (2009a) Towards an identity-based brand equity model, *Journal of Business Research*, **62** (3), pp. 390–97

Burmann, C and Zeplin, S (2005) Building brand commitment: A behavioural approach to internal brand management, *Journal of Brand Management*, **12** (4), pp. 279–300

Burmann, C, Zeplin, S and Riley, N (2009b) Key determinants of internal brand management success: An exploratory empirical analysis, *Journal of Brand Management*, **16** (4), pp. 264–84

Campbell, J P and Pritchard, R D (1976) Motivation theories in industrial and organizational psychology, in Dunnette, M D (ed), *Handbook of Industrial and Organizational Psychology*, Chicago: Rand McNally, pp. 63–130

Cyert, R M and March, J G (1963) *A Behavioral Theory of the Firm*, Englewood Cliffs: Prentice-Hall

Du Preez, R and Bendixen, M T (2015) The impact of internal brand management on employee job satisfaction, brand commitment and intention to stay, *International Journal of Bank Marketing*, **33** (1), pp. 78–91

Henkel, S, Tomczak, T, Heitmann, M and Herrmann, A (2007) Managing brand consistent employee behaviour: Relevance and managerial control of behavioural branding, *Journal of Product & Brand Management*, **16** (5), pp. 310–20

Homburg, C and Pflesser, C (2000) A multiple-layer model of market-oriented organizational culture: Measurement issues and performance outcomes, *Journal of Marketing Research*, **37** (4), pp. 449–62

Iglesias, O, Ind, N and Alfaro, M (2013) The organic view of the brand: A brand value co-creation model, *Journal of Brand Management*, **20** (8), pp. 670–88

Ind, N (2007), *Living the Brand: How to transform every member of your organization into a brand champion*, 3rd edn., London: Kogan Page

Ind, N (2014) How participation is changing the practice of managing brands, *Journal of Brand Management*, **21** (9), pp. 734–42

Ind, N, Iglesias, O and Schultz, M (2013) Building brands together, *California Management Review*, **55** (3), pp. 5–26

Keller, K L (1999) Brand mantras: Rational, criteria and examples, *Journal of Marketing Management*, **15** (1–3), pp. 43–51

King, C and Grace, D (2010) Building and measuring employee-based brand equity, *European Journal of Marketing*, **44** (7/8), pp. 938–71

Kraus, T, Seifert, J and Blankenfeldt, L (2007) Markenführung bei TNT (Brand management at TNT), in Schmidt, H J (ed), *Internal Branding*, Wiesbaden: Gabler, pp. 133–51

Mahnert, K F and Torres, A M (2007) The brand inside: The factors of failure and success in internal branding, *Irish Marketing Review*, **19** (1/2), p. 54

Morhart, F M, Herzog, W and Tomczak, T (2009) Brand-specific leadership: Turning employees into brand champions, *Journal of Marketing*, **73** (5), pp. 122–42

Napoli, J (2006) The impact of nonprofit brand orientation on organisational performance, *Journal of Marketing Management*, **22** (7–8), pp. 673–94

Noble, C H, Sinha, R K and Kumar, A (2002) Market orientation and alternative strategic orientations: A longitudinal assessment of performance implications, *Journal of Marketing*, **66** (4), pp. 25–39

Patagonia (2016) Patagonia's Mission Statement [online] http://www.patagonia.com/company-info.html [accessed 29 October 2016]

Petty, R E and Cacioppo, J T (1986) The elaboration likelihood model of persuasion, *Advances in Experimental Social Psychology*, **19**, pp. 123–62

Phan, M, Thomas, R and Heine, K (2011) Social media and luxury brand management: The case of Burberry, *Journal of Global Fashion Marketing*, **2** (4), pp. 213–22

Rosenstiel, L V (2003) *Grundlagen der Organisationspsychologie (Basics of Organizational Psychology), Sammlung Poeschel*, Vol. 95, 5th edn., Stuttgart: Schäffer-Poeschel

Saleem, F Z and Iglesias, O (2016) Mapping the domain of the fragmented field of internal branding, *Journal of Product & Brand Management*, **25** (1), pp. 43–57

Schein, E H (2006) *Organizational Culture and Leadership*, New York: John Wiley & Sons

Schmidt, H J and Baumgarth, C (2014) Introducing a conceptual model of brand orientation within the context of Social Entrepreneurial Businesses, *International Journal of Strategic Innovative Marketing*, **1** (1), pp. 37–50

Schmidt, H J, Baumgarth, C, Wiedmann, K-P and Lückenbach, F (2015) Strategic orientations and the performance of Social Entrepreneurial Organisations (SEOs): A conceptual model, *Social Business*, **5** (2), pp. 131–55

Schuler, H and Moser, K (eds.) (2014) *Organisationspsychologie (Organisational Psychology)*, 5th edn., Bern: Hans Huber

Schunk, D H (2012) *Learning Theories: An educational perspective*, 6th edn, Pearson, Boston

Seifert, J and Schmidt, H J (2006) Der transportierte Markenwert (The transported brand value), *Personalwirtschaft*, **11**, pp. 34–36

Thomson, K, Chernatony, L de, Arganbright, L and Khan, S (1999 The buy-in benchmark: How staff understanding and commitment impact brand and business performance, *Journal of Marketing Management*, **15** (8), pp. 819–35

Urde, M (1994) Brand orientation: A strategy for survival, *Journal of Consumer Marketing*, **11** (3), pp. 18–32

Urde, M (1999) Brand orientation: A mindset for building brands into strategic resources, *Journal of Marketing Management*, **15** (1–3), pp. 117–33

Urde, M, Baumgarth, C and Merrilees, B (2013) Brand orientation and market orientation: From alternatives to synergy, *Journal of Business Research*, **66** (1), pp. 13–20

Vroom, V H (1964), *Work and Motivation*, New York: Wiley

Wentzel, D, Tomczak, T, Kernstock, J, Brexendorf, T O and Henkel, S (2014) Den Funnel als Analyse- und Steuerungsinstrument von Brand Behavior heranziehen (Using the funnel as instrument for analysis and regulation of brand behavior), in Esch, F-R, Tomczak, T, Kernstock, J, Langner, T and Redler, J (eds.) *Corporate Brand Management: Marken als Anker strategischer Führung von Unternehmen*, 3rd edn, Wiesbaden: Springer Gabler, pp. 227–41

Yin Wong, H and Merrilees, B (2008) The performance benefits of being brand-orientated, *Journal of Product & Brand Management*, **17** (6), pp. 372–83

Unleashing the internal fan community through brand-oriented leadership

03

FELICITAS MORHART

Every brand-driven company dreams about having a brand community (Fournier *et al.*, 2000; Muniz Jr and O'Guinn, 2001) – a community of devoted customers worshipping their brand and renouncing competitor brands. Think of those avid Apple evangelists, iconic Harley Davidson riders, passionate Nutella lovers, and audacious GoPro athletes. Whether or not a brand has community potential has a lot to do with the brand itself at the centre of the community. The brand needs to offer meaning, identification, and enable social life. However, in the first place every brand is crafted by company leaders and brought to life through the people representing it at customer touch points. Leaders of a company need to unleash their brand's internal community potential and turn employees into fans first, before the employees can turn customers into fans. But how can leaders unleash this potential and turn employees into fans of the brand?

Based on the author's research (see Morhart, 2008, Morhart *et al.*, 2009 and Morhart *et al.*, 2011) as well as her training and consulting experience, this chapter provides (1) insights and recommendations for managers who want to turn their employees into brand champions, (2) ideas for trainers who are in charge of brand-oriented leadership development inside their companies, and (3) a point of departure for researchers who want to take research on brand-oriented leadership further.

Employee brand-oriented behaviour

When we talk about turning employees into brand champions, we first need to clarify what managers can hope to achieve. Strictly speaking, managers can aim to make their employees contribute (both on and off the job) to the organization's brand-oriented efforts. Employees' brand-oriented behaviour can take two forms (apart from merely staying employed with the brand (Morhart *et al.*, 2009)): brand-supportive and brand-strengthening behaviour.

Brand-supportive behaviour

This type of behaviour refers to employees acting consistently and dependably in line with the standards prescribed by their role as brand representatives. Such standards are sometimes stipulated in behavioural codices, manuals, or display rules. The aim of setting behavioural stand-ards is to secure a brand experience for customers which is consistent with the brand promise conveyed through the organization's public brand messages. A fast food chain offering a 'smile guarantee' raises customers' expectation that they will receive their burger and fries with a smile, a friendly gesture, and maybe an uplifting comment (see for example McDonald's guarantee: 'If we don't smile before you pay you get a free small French Fries or Hash Brown' (Hennig-Thurau and Paul, 2007)). If employees are not able to fulfil those customer expec-tations raised by the brand promise, customers are likely to respond with dissatisfaction or even defection (Berry, 2000). In that sense, brand-supportive employee behaviour should be considered a 'must-have' which, if not met, leads to customers' dissatisfaction.

Brand-strengthening behaviour

This type of behaviour can be considered real fandom, because it is behaviour which is not prescribed by company rules, but is voluntary. Brand-strengthening behaviour refers to employees' discretionary actions for the good of the brand. Two categories of such 'extra-role' behaviour are particularly valuable. The first one, *participation in brand development*, refers to employees internally passing on brand-relevant customer feedback from touch points in order to inform brand management about improvement potential. As such, they provide the company with input which is possibly of higher quality and less expensive than that provided by market research. The second one, *positive word of mouth*, refers to employees' personal advocacy of the brand outside the job context. It is a proven fact that peer-to-peer recommendations are a far more credible and powerful form of advertising than any form of company-issued communication (Nielsen, 2015). By having employees promote the brand in their personal surroundings, a company creates a highly effective means of customer acquisition which, at the same time, also saves a considerable amount of advertising spending. Brand-strengthening behaviours go beyond brand-supportive behaviours insofar that they not only help secure the brand's image and equity, but help increase it.

Leadership styles to foster brand-oriented behaviour

With respect to the differentiation between prescribed (brand-supportive) and voluntary (brand-strengthening) employee behaviours, Bass's (1985) theory of transactional and transformational leadership proves to be particularly useful. As we will see in the following section, transactional leaders act differently from transformational leaders and activate different psychological processes on the part of their employees which in turn trigger different brand-oriented behaviours.

Brand-specific transactional leadership (TRL)

TRL is founded on the idea that leader–follower relations are based on a series of exchanges or implicit bargains. Following a 'tit-for-tat' logic, followers receive certain valued outcomes on the condition that they act according to their leader's expectations. As such, this leadership style mainly works through employees' *extrinsic motivation*. Transactional leaders set goals and issue instructions, they define processes and conditions, and exert control by monitoring mistakes or deviance from prescribed standards. Depending on employees' performance, they offer rewards or impose punishments. The duality of positive contingent reinforcement (*Contingent Reward*) and negative contingent reinforcement/corrective action (*Management by Exception*) forms the core composition of transactional leadership.

Let us apply this concept to the present context of internal branding. A manager who aims to strengthen their employees' brand-oriented behaviours by means of a *transactional leadership style*:

- sets behavioural standards defining how employees should act out their role as brand representatives and offers rewards when role expectations are met;
- closely monitors employees' compliance with behavioural standards as brand representatives and takes corrective and punishing action in case of employees' deviance, mistakes, and errors.

This kind of leadership style is prevalent in firms that attach a lot of importance to standardized services in order to ensure a consistent and coherent presentation at customer touch points. For example, a German retailer had translated its brand values of 'freshness', 'competence', 'responsibility' and 'controlled quality' into concrete behavioural guidelines for its employees at fresh food counters. Through performance control instruments, such as mystery shopping, managers could monitor frontline employees' compliance with the standards.

Pros

Transactional leadership has a variety of positive effects, which is why it is generally considered an effective and necessary leadership style (Lowe *et al.*, 1996). Transactional leaders clarify roles, tasks, and performance expectations for employees. This in turn creates transparency and is conducive to an atmosphere of trust, fairness, and security, in which employees know what they need to do to fulfil leaders' expectations.

Cons

Clear behavioural standards and close monitoring are very likely to lead to a highly reliable and uniform demeanour of employees at customer touch points. However, chances are that while performing their prescribed roles, employees' behaviour appears inauthentic and over-rehearsed, if not robot-like. Remember the smile guarantee that was mentioned earlier. How genuine is an employee's smile likely to be when they hand you over your order? And how likely are you to smile back? Transactional leadership has its limits when it comes to the display of emotions. When a role is externally imposed (in contrast to naturally adopted), employees might be able to 'play' that role, but they are not able to 'live' it, which might lead to inferior 'surface acting' (Hennig-Thurau *et al.*, 2006). Furthermore, rules and scripts can easily become a corset curtailing employees' spontaneity, flexibility, and true emotional expression in their role enactment, which can lead to feelings of inauthenticity, self-alienation, and burnout (Yagil and Medler-Liraz, 2014).

Certainly, in the context of employee branding efforts, transactional leadership does have its place. Particularly in the early stages of a company-wide brand engagement programme, it is advisable to clarify employees' roles as brand representatives by means of clear instructions and behavioural rules. Having a concrete idea about what constitutes effective brand-representing behaviour, employees are better equipped to include such (new) role behaviour in their extant set of job role behaviours and to provide a coherent and consistent brand presence at customer touch points. With regard to the difference between brand-supportive and brand-strengthening behaviour, brand-specific transactional leadership specifically targets employees' brand-supportive behaviours.

Brand-specific transformational leadership (TFL)

According to this leadership style's name, TFL aims at transforming employees' motives and goals for the good of the whole company. In this leadership paradigm, short-term individualistic (or even egoistic) goals give way to long-term, higher-order values and objectives. Transformational leaders aim at emotionally involving their employees in order to facilitate identification, commitment and trust in their mission. Hence, TFL mainly works through employees' *intrinsic motivation*. Leaders mobilize their teams by imparting an attractive and meaningful vision, by convincingly showing how common goals can be jointly achieved, by acting as a role model, and by supporting employees' intellectual and personal development. These leadership behaviours form the four main components of transformational leadership: *Inspirational Motivation, Idealized Influence, Intellectual Stimulation,* and *Individualized Consideration.*

Let us think this through in the context of internal branding: a manager who aims to strengthen their employees' brand-oriented behaviours by means of a *transformational leadership style*:

- articulates a compelling and differentiating brand vision that rouses personal involvment, enthusiasm, and employees' pride in the brand;
- acts as a role model by authentically living the brand values and promise in daily work life;
- encourages employees to reframe their jobs from the perspective of a brand representative, and empowers and helps them to interpret the brand promise and its implications for their work in light of their individual job profiles;
- teaches and coaches employees to grow into their roles as representatives of the brand.

One company that showcases brand-oriented transformational leadership culture in action is the world famous Ritz Carlton hotel group. Their credo, 'We are ladies and gentlemen serving ladies and gentlemen', stands for respect – not only towards customers, but in particular towards employees who are not supposed to feel like the guests' servants, but like hosts with style and dignity (Michaelsen, 2011). In this vein, management appeals to employees' pride and self-esteem and as such conveys meaning and identification (*Inspirational Motivation*). Furthermore, Ritz Carlton has institutionalized a culture of independent and creative thinking (*Intellectual Stimulation*): each employee has the mission to render a guest's stay an unforgettable experience. For this purpose, Ritz Carlton allows each employee, whatever their position, to spend up to US\$ 2,000 per incident in order to solve independently a guest's problem or to bestow a 'wow moment' on a guest (a collection of 'wow stories' about employees who independently created extraordinary customer experiences can be found on the website of the hotel's proprietary leadership centre, **http://ritzcarltonleadershipcenter.com/category/ guest-stories/**). In this way, management transfers responsibility for the brand to each and every organizational member. Furthermore, to enable employees to deliver on the brand promise within the scope of their job profiles and according to their talents and skills, management has established comprehensive training and individual coaching (*Individual Consideration*). (See Ritz Carlton's 'Employee Promise': 'We nurture and maximize talent to the benefit of each individual and the company.') Ritz Carlton's brand-oriented transformational leadership culture is completed by its managers, whose mission is to spread the 'Ritz spirit' among employees and hence to instil pride, ownership of the brand, and responsibility for its well-being. The hotel chain's founder, Horst Schulze, always believed in true leadership in terms of role modelling (*Idealized Influence*): 'A *manager* who spots a cigarette butt in the flower bed chews the gardener out. A *leader* picks up the butt, throws it into the bin and asks the gardener what needs to be done to avoid this happening in the future' (Michaelsen, 2011).

Pros

International research (Den Hartog *et al.*, 1999) defines transformational and charismatic leadership as the epitome of excellent people management. Several studies have shown a positive relation between TFL and various subjective and objective performance criteria (see, for example, the meta-analytic reviews by Fuller *et al.*, 1996 or Lowe *et al.*, 1996). Furthermore, TFL's positive influence on attitudinal and behavioural criteria such as employee satisfaction, commitment, identification, and organizational citizenship has been shown consistently (Kark *et al.*, 2003; Podsakoff *et al.*, 1996). In contrast to TRL, which relies on employees' instrumental compliance, TFL works through a process of internalization on the part of employees (Kark *et al.*, 2003; Kelman, 1958; MacKenzie, *et al.*, 2001). In the present context this means that employees of a brand-oriented transformational leader fully take on their role as representatives of the brand by integrating this brand-related role identity into their self-concepts. In the process, employees come to accept the brand values as their own and therefore perceive value congruence between their own and the brand's values (for example, when a bank's promise 'true to you' becomes a central facet in a trader's personal code of conduct). Thus brand ambassadorship becomes a natural expression of employees' selves, which guides behaviour in various situations (not only in pre-defined standard situations) and can be transferred into new and different contexts. Put differently, brand ambassadorship is not about playing a role, but living it and interpreting and adapting it situatively. As TFL transforms employees' concept of self, it not only leads to brand-supportive employee behaviour but also to brand-strengthening behaviour – reinforcing a human tendency to self-affirm and self-enhance (see also Shamir *et al.*, 1993). Employees who have integrated their role as brand representatives into their self-concepts are motivated to engage in extra efforts to strengthen the image of the brand to which their own identity is tied. As such, actions for the good of the brand such as positive word of mouth and active engagement in brand development are closely tied to employees' self-esteem and are therefore self-motivated.

Cons

At times, TFL can overcharge employees; new employees in particular might not be able to deal with the large amount of autonomy and responsibility that is granted to them, and end up clueless about how to translate the global brand vision into concrete action. In addition, the aspect of intellectual stimulation might lead to employees' feeling uncertain, pressured, and unconfident when they are constantly asked to challenge the current way of doing things and to search for improvements (MacKenzie *et al.*, 2001). Here, it is the leader's task to assist and coach employees in their individual development. In addition, chances are that employees develop strong attachment to their transformational leader, which might develop into dysfunctional dependency (Kark *et al.*, 2003). If the leader leaves the organization, employees can feel helpless and lack a clear orientation. Particularly in the context of brand-oriented leadership, managers need to actively channel the emotional commitment they trigger in employees, so that employees do not identify only with the person but first and foremost with the brand. This latter aspect is also a crucial differentiator between positive transformational leadership as described here, and dysfunctional 'pseudo'-tranformational leadership (Bass and Steidlmeier 1999). In the case of pseudo-transformational leadership, the leader misuses his charismatic effects for self-interest in his striving for power and/or narcissistic self-adulation. Against this background, brand-oriented transformational leadership demands a careful balancing act to avoid employee manipulation or indoctrination.

Brand engagement programmes which aim to implement employees' brand behaviour company-wide entail a process of fundamental change. When it comes to the transformation of a whole organization towards brand orientation, transformational leadership is the approach of choice. As mentioned earlier, brand-specific TRL can help to bring about first changes in employees' visible behaviour and therefore help to kick off incremental change (*1st order change*). However, a fully-fledged brand-oriented transformation process demands a fundamental shift of mindest in the whole organization (*2nd order change*). Transformational leaders can help employees to perform the necessary change of perspective so that they can see their jobs through the lens of a brand representative in the future. Here, transformational leaders act as sense makers by re-interpreting the company's goal and value system in light of the brand's vision. Employees are then able to discern meaning in their role as brand representatives and internalize this new role step by step so that it ultimately shapes their daily sensing, thinking, and feeling in a natural way.

To summarize, both brand-specific TRL and brand-specific TFL have their merits and their risks. Before employing one or the other style, managers need to be aware of the different motivational processes that each of these styles activates in employees resulting in different behavioural outcomes. Depending on the context and goals the manager wants to achieve, TFL might be more appropriate than TRL or vice versa. Hence, a situational analysis is recommended before resorting to one or the other leadership style. For example, due to the concreteness of instructions a transactional leader gives and the clarity about desirable and undesirable behaviour they provide, TRL might be appropriate in situations when standardized brand behaviour is desirable at customer touch points and when such behaviour is standardizable. Furthermore, TRL might be more appropriate than TFL in the early stages of a brand engagement programme when employees are not yet familiar and flexible enough to interpret the brand vision in their own ways, or when employees are immature or new to the company and so need guidance and structure. Here, employees' mere compliance with behavioural standards might be sufficient to secure a consistent and reliable brand experience. However, the more complex and variable the context for brand behaviour, such as in highly individualized service settings or settings high in emotional labour, the less standardization is desirable and possible. In addition, the more mature and adept employees are in their role as brand representatives, the higher the risk that employees feel coerced and patronized by managers. In these latter cases, TFL is more appropriate as it allows employees to live the brand in individual ways and empowers them to take ownership of the brand and its further development. Thus, each leadership style's limits appear to be the strength of the other, and managers need to concert them carefully to effectively manage brand behaviour.

The following figure summarizes the discussion about the employee impact of the psychological processes and behavioural outcomes of brand-specific TRL and TFL as well as their context-specific applicability.

In order to help managers choose a specific leadership style in a given situation, the following checklist provides a decision aid.

Figure 3.1   The operation of brand-specific transactional and transformational leadership

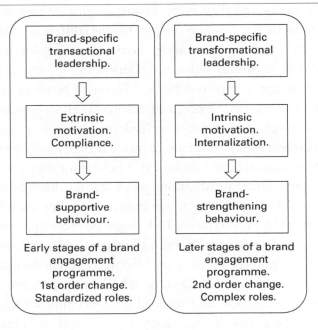

Table 3.1   Decision aid for situative choice of brand-specific leadership style

	Brand-specific transactional leadership	Brand-specific transformational leadership
Objective	Employees represent the brand at customer touch points in a uniform and reliable manner	Employees live the brand in their own ways and take spontaneous initiative on behalf of the brand
Scope/stage of brand engagement programme	Narrow scope (limited to some functions); early stage of engagement programme	Company-wide scope; later stages of engagement programme
Employee job profile	Easily definable, standardized tasks	Complex, varying tasks
Employee maturity	New, immature	Experienced, mature

Becoming a brand-specific transformational leader

From the author's own consulting and training experience it has become clear that managers mainly resort to the transactional leadership approach. This is due to several reasons. First, TRL is easier to learn and apply. For example, specifying behavioural codices and scripts for employees dealing with customers and then monitoring and rewarding appropriate demeanour is a straightforward task. In contrast, devising a compelling vision and being inspiring is far more demanding. Indeed, many managers think that transformational or charismatic leadership is a gift of god that cannot be learned ('leaders are born, not made' is a phrase often heard by seminar participants). Second, TRL leads to predictable outcomes, because objectives are cleary defined, and results show quickly due to the desired behaviour's coupling with rewards. On the other hand, TFL works with a more abstract vision and higher-order objectives that encourage followers' own interpretation and initiative, which might lead to unexpected outcomes. Furthermore, as TFL gives precedence to long-term objectives over short-term goals, results sometimes take longer to show – oftentimes too long for managers pressured by quarterly reports. Third, transactional leaders have objectives, processes, and structures that do the leading job for them, while transformational leaders have to invest a lot of their personal time and energy to challenge, coach, and develop their employees.

Hence, although most managers agree on their companies' need for more transformational leadership, they share a tremendous lack of knowledge and ability in this leadership style (to assess your own brand-specific leadership see the Brand-Specific TFL Quick Check below). In order to help managers apply brand-specific leadership in practice, the author and her colleagues developed a specific management training programme and successfully evaluated its effectiveness by means of a rigorous field experiment (Morhart *et al.*, 2009). The study showed that a training and coaching intervention can significantly improve managers' brand-specific transformational leadership style as perceived by their subordinates within just a few months. Who said that leaders are just born?

The following decribes the training programme's format, contents, and techniques and gives chief learning officers, heads of talent development, and trainers ideas for the creation of their own brand-oriented leadership development programmes.

Brand-Specific TFL Quick Check

1 To what extent do I convincingly communicate a compelling and differentiating brand vision so that employees are enthusiastic and proud of our brand?

2 To what extent do I deliver on our brand promise? To what extent am I an authentic role model when it comes to our brand values?

3 To what extent do I engage in meaning management in the sense that I help employees think beyond their job profiles and reframe their tasks from the perspective of someone responsible for the brand?

4 To what extent do I assist and coach my own employees in their development as brand champions?

Group-based training

The training is designed as a two-day off-site workshop with an optimal group size of 15 to 20 participants. Approximately two weeks before the training, participants should fill in the brand-specific multifactor leadership questionnaire (brand-specific MLQ) (Morhart, 2008; Morhart *et al.*, 2011) in order to assess managers' self-perception of their level of brand-specific transformational leadership. The questionnaire should also be administered to managers' subordinates in order to obtain other reports on managers' level of brand-specific transformational leadership. By the time of the training, survey results should have been analysed and visualized in the form of an aggregate report so that it can be presented to managers.

The training itself is inspired by Bass and Avolio's (1999) Full Range Leadership Development programme and a self-management training programme developed by Storch and Krause (2002). Regarding means of knowledge transfer techniques, this training uses a blend of input lectures, examples, case analysis, interactive group discussion, as well as individual and team exercises. The two-day programme is structured in five parts.

Part 1

The first part is essentially about setting the stage for participants. Here, a member of the top management team should explain to the group in person the need for the training and its embedding in the company's overall strategic marketing efforts. This part should not be underestimated as participants oftentimes come to a brand-oriented leadership training session with a good deal of skepticism – especially if they are from functions that are remote from marketing and branding. The signalling of top management commitment is a crucial act of symbolic (and transformational!) leadership which can make or break participants' commitment and engagement throughout the rest of the training.

Part 2

In the second part, participants become familiar with the central concept of brand-specific transformational leadership as compared to brand-specific transactional leadership. This part of the programme can be kick-started by a case study exercise that illustrates a successful internal brand engagement programme and leaders' role in it, and which identifies parallels with participants' own situation (for potential case studies, readers might draw from examples featured in this book). The case study exercise should include small group assignments with subsequent presentation and discussion in the plenum. The final debriefing by the facilitator should mark the transition to the input lecture which should cover theory, research findings, and best and worst practice examples drawn from different domains such as business, sports, music, history and education. Transformational leadership role models do not always have to be real characters; they can also be sourced from fiction and movies such as the famous *Dead Poets Society*.

Part 3

Equipped with this knowledge, managers are ready to think about the desired brand-oriented future of their own company. In small groups, managers should elaborate leadership principles that would help to bring the organization's brand vision to life. Concretely, teams should work on four leadership principles – one for each of the components of brand-specific transformational leadership – to help employees live the brand and deliver on the company's brand promise. Each team's proposal should be presented and discussed in the plenum. Afterwards, each manager should work on their own to create their individual brand-specific leadership vision. Thereby, each manager's individual vision should fulfil the following three criteria (Storch and Krause, 2002): it should be formulated positively (ie in terms of an approach instead of an avoidance goal); it should be attainable (even if only in the long term); and it should be personally attractive, evoking positive feelings in the manager (and hopefully also in their employees). Participants should verbalize their vision in a written statement and then visualize it by means of a personal collage. In order to make managers feel at ease with this exercise, it is suggested to situate it in a relaxed and easygoing atmosphere with music, food, and drinks. This part is the end of the first training day.

Part 4

In this part, the aggregated group-level results from the leadership assessment conducted prior to the training should be presented.

Thereby, managers' self-evaluated leadership should be contrasted with their subordinates' evaluation. This session is a neuralgic point in the training, because it acts as an eye-opener to participants when it comes to the discrepancies between their self-perception and their subordinates' perceptions of their leadership abilities. Hence, facilitation skills and a great deal of sensitivity are demanded from the trainer. Results should be interpreted and discussed in the plenum; strengths and weaknesses should be identified together and synthesized by means of a gap analysis. Subsequently, managers should split into small groups to devise concrete actions to reduce the identified gaps. More specifically, teams should be asked to define behaviours and measures with which they could foster brand-specific transformational leadership in their everyday work life. Again, the teams' suggestions should be presented and vetted in the plenum.

Part 5

The last part of the two-day training should be devoted to preparing participants' transfer of the acquired knowledge into their daily routine back in the office. Here, trainers can resort to self-management literature (eg Bruch and Ghoshal, 2002; Storch and Krause, 2002). Exercises should prepare participants to anticipate future failues, monitor past and present failures, and build up a rich pool of resources (visual cues, reminders, symbols, buddies, etc.) to cope with future risky situations (risky in the sense of falling back into old routines). Finally, managers can be asked to write a 'letter to myself' in which they should formulate their commitment to themselves regarding their objective of becoming a more brand-specific transformational leader. This letter should be sent to participants approximately four weeks after the training as a 'litmus test' of their personal progress.

Personal coaching

In order to increase training effectiveness, it is recommended to supplement the two-day training with individual coaching sessions approximately one month later. That is, each manager who has participated in the training should be invited to a 1.5-hour, one-on-one meeting either with a specialized coach or the trainer. In preparation for this session, each manager should receive their personalized brand-specific MLQ feedback report in advance. The format of this individual report should mirror the aggregate report of the initial training so that managers can work through and interpret the data privately on their own before the meeting. The coaching session should be devoted to discussing the coachees' personal leadership vision, the strengths, weaknesses, and discrepancies between self versus subordinates' ratings from the feedback report, as well as opportunities for personal improvement on the way to brand-specific transformational leadership excellence. Each manager should define two to three leadership aspects that they want to improve, which should then be translated into a concrete action plan for the following months. Potential obstacles to the plan's implementation should also be identified and coping resources for relapse prevention should be identified.

Conclusion

Brand-specific leadership is not a 'one size fits all' exercise. To turn employees into fans and have them bring the brand to life at customer touch points, managers need to carefully orchestrate different leadership styles according to the desired outcomes, context, and employee situation. At times, a transactional leadership style might suffice, for example when circumstances call for a standardized, efficient approach to secure a coherent and reliable representation of the brand at customer touch points. When placing your command at the drive-in counter of a fast food chain, a standardized behaviour script executed by a person in a branded uniform probably does the trick – even more so because efficiency and reliability are likely part of the brand's identity. However, a hospital brand giving its patients the promise that 'we truly care for you' demands much more from brand representatives. Here, employees need to identify with their role as care givers and need to truly believe in the brand's mission in order to show the empathy and sensitivity necessary to make patients feel taken care of as promised. In this case, brand-specific TFL is the leadership style of choice, as leaders will have to engage employees deeply in internalizing the job role into self-conceptions.

It is the author's hope that through this chapter (1) managers can develop an understanding of the different leadership styles they have at their disposal, as well as the when and how of their use, to turn their employees into effective brand champions, (2) trainers can better understand how to create brand-specific leadership development programmes, and (3) researchers are inspired to take the exciting domain of internal branding further.

References

Bass, B M (1985) *Leadership and Performance Beyond Expectations*, New York: The Free Press

Bass, B M and Avolio, B J (1999) *Training Full Range Leadership: A resource guide for training with the MLQ*, Redwood City: Mind Garden

Bass, B M and Steidlmeier, P (1999) Ethics, character, and authentic transformational leadership behaviour, *Leadership Quarterly*, **10** (2), pp. 181–217

Berry, L L (2000) Cultivating service brand equity, *Journal of the Academy of Marketing Science*, **28** (1), pp. 128–37

Bruch, H and Ghoshal, S (2002) Beware the busy manager, *Harvard Business Review*, **80** (2), pp. 62–69

Den Hartog, D N, House, R, Hanges, P J, Ruiz-Quintanilla, S A and Dorfman, P W (1999) Culture specific and cross-culturally generalizable implicit leadership theories: Are attributes of charismatic/transformational leadership universally endorsed? *Leadership Quarterly*, **10** (2), pp. 219–56

Fournier, S, McAlexander, J, Schouten, J and Sensiper, S (2000) *Building Brand Community on the Harley-Davidson Posse Ride*, Harvard Business School Publishing.

Fuller, J B, Patterson, C E P, Hester, K and Stringer, D Y (1996) A quantitative review of research on charismatic leadership, *Psychological Reports*, **78**, pp. 271–87

Hennig-Thurau, T, Groth, M, Paul, M and Gremler, D D (2006) Are all smiles created equal? How emotional contagion and emotional labor affect service relationships, *Journal of Marketing*, **70** (3), pp. 58–73

Hennig-Thurau, T and Paul, M (2007) Mitarbeiteremotionen als steuerungsgröße des dienstleistungserfolges, in: Gouthier, M H J, C Coenen, H S Schulze and C Wegmann (eds.), *Service Excellence als Impulsgeber: Strategien – management – innovationen – branchen*, 1st edn, Wiesbaden: Gabler, pp. 363–82

Kark, R, Shamir, B, and Chen, G (2003) The two faces of transformational leadership: Empowerment and dependency, *Journal of Applied Psychology*, 88 (2), pp. 246–55

Kelman, H C (1958) Compliance, identification, and internalization: Three processes of attitude change, *The Journal of Conflict Resolution*, 2 (1), pp. 51–60

Lowe, K B, Kroeck, K G and Sivasubramaniam, N (1996), Effectiveness correlates of transformational and transactional leadership: A meta-analytic review of the MLQ literature, *Leadership Quarterly*, 7 (3), pp. 385–425

MacKenzie, S B, Podsakoff, P M and Rich, G A (2001) Transformational and transactional leadership and salesperson performance, *Journal of the Academy of Marketing Science*, 29 (2), 115–34

Michaelsen, S (2011) Sex-Wünsche – 'Wir verweisen auf die Gelben Seiten', *Welt* [online] http://www.welt.de/reise/article12447973/Sex-Wuensche-Wir-verweisen-auf-die-Gelben-Seiten.html [accessed 13 May 2016]

Morhart, F (2008) *Brand-specific Leadership: on its effects and trainability*, Saarbrücken: Südwestdeutscher Verlag für Hochschulschriften

Morhart, F M, Herzog, W and Tomczak, T (2009) Brand-specific leadership: Turning employees into brand champions, *Journal of Marketing*, 73 (5), pp. 122–42

Morhart, F M, Herzog, W and Tomczak, T (2011) Turning employees into brand champions: Leadership style makes a difference *GfK Marketing Intelligence Review*, 3 (2), 34–43

Muniz Jr, A M and O'Guinn, T C (2001) Brand community, *Journal of Consumer Research*, 27 (4), pp. 412–32

Nielsen (2015) *Global Trust in Advertising*, The Nielsen Company

Podsakoff, P M, MacKenzie, S B, and Bommer, W H (1996) Transformational leader behaviors and substitutes for leadership as determinants of employee satisfaction, commitment, trust, and organizational citizenship behaviors, *Journal of Management*, 22 (2), pp. 259–98

Shamir, B, House, R J, and Arthur, M B (1993). The motivational effects of charismatic leadership: A self-concept based theory. *Organization Science*, 4(4), 577–594

Storch, M and Krause, F (2002) *Selbstmanagement – ressourcenorientiert: Grundlagen und trainingsmanual für die arbeit mit dem zürcher ressourcen modell*, Bern: Huber

Yagil, D and Medler-Liraz, H (2014) Feel free, be yourself: Authentic leadership, emotional expression, and employee authenticity, *Journal of Leadership and Organizational Studies*, 21 (1), pp. 59–70

Bond Dickinson: 04 leading by example

ERIKA UFFINDELL

Introduction

As a brand consultant, I have had the privilege of being involved in many 'Living the Brand' programmes over the last 25 years for organizations across a wide range of sectors. Some have been more successful than others, and in my view the difference between success and failure results from one word: leadership.

If leaders aren't fully involved in the process or if they delegate the delivery of the programme to a function within the business, the programme rarely gets the full traction, engagement and commitment it deserves.

Companies often invest in outside agencies or consultancies to define the brand or run numerous values workshops and then fall down when it comes to the embedding process. It often becomes a simple 'tell' process and at worse a 'brand book' arrives on an employee's desk for them to digest at their leisure (if they have any!) or a screen saver pops up on their desk top with a series of Values and the employee is left to wonder what they are supposed to do with them.

However, those companies that realize the importance of their senior people leading this process and the value of providing an integrated story for their people around their Vision, Brand and Culture, are the ones that reap the greatest rewards.

Bond Dickinson, a leading UK law firm, is one such company. They undertook a 'Living the Brand' programme, and in doing so, demonstrated the importance both of leadership and of taking an integrated and holistic view of where and how brand fits into an organization.

Following a merger of two companies, Bond Dickinson set out in 2014 to clearly articulate its vision, desired culture and brand promise. They regarded these three elements as interdependent and therefore took an integrated approach to their development and introduction.

What follows is the case study of the Bond Dickinson programme, outlining the approach they took, their learning and the outcomes achieved.

Background to the firm

Bond Dickinson is a UK national law firm with international alliances. The firm was created through a 2012 merger of two regional law firms, Bond Pearce and Dickinson Dees. The firm is a partnership and has 130 partners, approximately 600 legal professionals and advises over 40 FTSE companies. It is also ranked 126 in the *Guardian* top 300 Employers of Choice. As part of the merger, and in addition to setting the strategy, the firm defined its vision, desired culture and a new brand platform to help build profile in the marketplace.

Setting up the approach – principles and mindset

Many mergers fail, not because of the strategy or opportunity but because leaders don't focus enough on the cultural alignment of the two firms.

Bond Dickinson recognized the importance of culture and the value of involving all of its people in the development and embedding of its vision, values and brand.

This approach was based on the premises that:

● when all employees are involved and have the opportunity to contribute to shaping the future of a firm, they are more fully engaged;

- when employees understand the relationship between the vision, culture and brand (the promise) of the firm they are more likely to understand their role in delivering that promise and feel a greater sense of fulfilment.

The Bond Dickinson executive team was already committed to a set of principles involving strong focus on people, open communication and teamwork. These were very much reflected in their overall approach to the process of embedding the vision and values and bringing the brand to life for their people.

As a part of the legal and cultural dynamics of a partnership, the firm needed, in any case, to provide the opportunity for partners to contribute to and approve the Vision of the firm. Bond Dickinson went one stage further. They expanded that thinking and approach to ensure that the firm as a whole was included in the development of the values and desired culture and adopted a fully interactive process for embedding the brand.

Developing the core elements in parallel

There were three core elements to this process that were developed in parallel – Vision, Values and Brand.

The Vision

Agreement to a far-reaching and effective Vision was seen as an essential precursor to development of the firm's strategy.

A draft of the vision was developed by the executive team and then distributed to a wider steering group for review. This process was highly interactive and provided the opportunity for debate and discussion.

The vision mapped out the high-level strategic ambitions of the firm and the imperatives, infrastructure and resources that would underpin the delivery.

The final draft of the vision was presented to the Partner group for agreement.

Involvement of: 130 partners.

The Values

In parallel to the development of the vision, the firm used the Barrett Values Centre Survey (a means of assessing personal and cultural values) as a way of offering everyone in the firm an opportunity to be involved in determining the ideal culture for the newly merged firm. The survey helped inform the selection of the core values that would drive the future culture of the firm.

They embraced a values-driven approach to determining the specific values that would drive culture and underpin delivery of the vision. The Barrett Values Survey offers a unique approach for a firm to understand:

- how aligned employees' personal values are with that of the firm;
- the gap between the current and desired culture – which gives leadership a focus for cultural change;
- the differences between business areas or geographies – which can provide indications of cultural nuances or differences in leadership/management styles;
- the different perspectives of new joiners compared to those who have been in the firm a long time.

In addition to informing the specific values that would best help to build a successful and sustainable firm, all these indicators helped provide critical information as to how best to evolve the culture and provide support and training to their people in a merger.

The Barrett Values Survey was sent out to all employees and had a 64 per cent response rate. Given that this was the first time the firm had run a firm-wide values survey, this was a very acceptable response. The Barrett Values Centre has found that the more consistently a firm involves its people in a survey of this nature (demonstrating its commitment), the higher the response rate.

Linking the Values to strategy and vision

Once the values survey information had been analysed and shared among the leadership team, a series of workshops was run in cross-practice and cross-functional teams to establish the resonance and relevancy of the values. The objective of these workshops was to establish the behaviours that best underpinned each value and to discuss the firm's ability to deliver on them.

The link back to strategy and vision was key here. The workshops explored and identified the values and behaviours that would best drive towards a successful execution of the strategy and the firm's ability to realize its vision.

The four core values were:

1 We put clients at the heart.

2 We value people.

3 We deliver excellence.

4 We work as one team.

Involvement of: Over 64 per cent of Bond Dickinson people.

The Brand

Third, and again as part of a parallel process, the brand platform was developed. The approach the firm took here was 'outside in, inside out'.

First they listened to their clients to understand their key drivers, challenges and opportunities and also their needs and expectations of a firm like Bond Dickinson. In a sector that has historically focused on, and invested in, delivering high-quality client service, there has been a general failure to build brands that reflect this. Instead they have focused their communication and marketing on 'what a law firm does', rather than 'the value it brings'.

Bond Dickinson understood there was an opportunity to create a brand that not only put clients front and centre in all they did but also accurately reflected this. Using the client insights, the firm ran a series of cross-practice brand forums to share the learning and discuss the implications and opportunities for the brand proposition and what the new firm should stand for.

It was clear that clients wanted a firm that listened first, that demonstrated knowledge and expertise in their sector, that was accessible and responsive, and perhaps most of all, really took the time to understand what mattered most to them. This could be a major shift in their strategy or marketplace, or a specific issue they had on, for example, intellectual property.

Whatever the issue, clients wanted their law firm to recognize the need and then work out how best to bring its insights, knowledge, expertise and resource to bear.

Aligned to this was the clients' perception of Bond Dickinson as a firm that was truly client focused and relationship driven. This empathetic approach and cultural strength was key in determining the final brand platform and organizing thought: 'What Matters Most'.

This new brand platform of 'What Matters Most' was defined as the promise that Bond Dickinson made to its clients and its people. It has served as a catalyst for some dynamic conversations to determine what matters most to these two key audiences and how Bond Dickinson can best serve their needs.

Involvement of: Over 100 people from across the firm.

A clear line of sight for employees: vision, values and brand

The opportunity to carry out these three work streams in parallel (Vision, Values, Brand) was a key part of the success of the Bond Dickinson programme. It enabled the firm to consistently align, adjust and back-check as the insights and ideas emerged and ensure coherence between the Vision, Values, Brand and the firm's strategy.

Too often, businesses develop and communicate their vision, values and brand in isolation. They therefore fail to provide their people with the important links or 'line of sight' they need to fully understand the role they can play in building the business.

To avoid this pitfall, Bond Dickinson took the important step of introducing the Vision, Values and Brand at the same time. And as part of this thinking they decided to:

- embed firm-wide – everyone would have the opportunity to personally attend a session where the vision, values and brand were introduced;

- design interactive sessions that ensured people not only understood the rationale for the development of these elements, but also experienced first-hand what it meant to deliver on them;

- ensure that the partners demonstrated commitment to the process by leading the embedding sessions;

- prototype the sessions to ensure relevance and resonance and adapt and enhance before rolling out;

- measure the response for understanding and engagement post-sessions;

- see this as a 'first step' to embedding the desired culture and brand and not 'the end of the process'.

Involving a cross-section of the firm in content and prototype

Before rolling out the three elements in these firm-wide embedding sessions, the executive team felt it was important to prototype the embedding sessions. Content was developed for a two-hour interactive session incorporating a mix of presentations and exercises. The sessions were designed to be co-facilitated by two of the partners and attended by approximately 20 participants.

Four prototype sessions were held in different Bond Dickinson office locations. Twelve people from across the business attended each session, including partners. At least one member of the executive team presented the content and co-facilitated the sessions.

Critical in this prototyping process was to ensure that the content and approach would be relevant and compelling for the breadth of people employed within Bond Dickinson.

Lessons were absorbed from the prototyping and the sessions were adapted prior to a session being run with the leadership team. This leadership team session comprised approximately 25 partners and members of the management committee and enabled the audiences to experience the sessions, give feedback and familiarize themselves with the content and the exercises. Many of those present at this session would go on to run the firm-wide embedding sessions.

Involvement of: Over 50 people across the firm.

Design and content of the sessions

The sessions comprised five sections:

1 **Welcome** and why this process was important to Bond Dickinson, including a video of the managing partner talking about the journey the firm had been on and why involving everyone in this process was key to the success of the firm.

2 **Vision** – an introduction to the vision and open discussion around what it meant for the individuals attending the sessions to help the firm deliver on this.

3 **Brand** – why brand was important, featuring an introduction to the new Bond Dickinson brand promise, including exercises on 'what matters most' to the clients of the firm.

4 **Values** – a summary of the findings from the Barrett Values Survey, introduction to the new values, 'what matters most' to the people of Bond Dickinson and exercises to establish to what degree people felt they were currently 'living out the values'.

5 **Summary and Q&A** – an opportunity for the facilitators to bring all the ideas and learning together and to open the session up for questions.

The sessions were designed to allow maximum time for people to share learning from the exercises and to hear their perspectives on what the firm was setting out to achieve.

Leading by example

Having developed the content, prototyped the sessions and run an initial leadership session it was time for the firm to roll out the sessions. The managing partner invited partners and leadership team members from across the business to volunteer to co-facilitate the sessions.

A total of 50 partners and leaders were then taken through a three-hour training session to ensure they were familiar with the content and exercises and had received basic facilitation training to support them in running the sessions.

They were also given a trainer's manual, which included:

- **Facilitator's guide** – a detailed guide of all the content and exercises.
- **Speaker notes** – key points to underpin the presentation.
- **Tips for facilitation** – best practice skills for facilitation.

Involvement of: 50 leaders including partners and members of the leadership team.

The embedding sessions – the rubber hits the road!

The embedding sessions ran over an eight-week period. Feedback from the sessions was captured and given to the Bond Dickinson HR team, who analysed it and gave their own feedback to the management team. Core to the success of the embedding sessions was achieving the right balance of information and active exercises. One of the core activities included was an active listening exercise. This required small groups of employees to listen to each other telling short stories that were personally meaningful for them. They then played back what they had heard around nuances between the more factual and emotional elements. During the development of the brand promise, 'What matters most', it became evident that a core capability in delivering the promise was to be able to 'actively listen to what clients and peers needed, expected and valued'. Including the active listening exercise within the embedding sessions helped people to experience and embody what it really meant to live out the brand promise and also added opportunities for personal development. One key learning for the firm in undertaking this exercise was that it was highly beneficial to have more than one person at key client meetings to ensure all aspects of the conversation were captured (vision, facts and emotions) and client needs ascertained.
Involvement of: All Bond Dickinson people.

Business as usual!

Part of the success of the programme was the understanding that this was the 'first step' on the journey of building a high-performing culture and brand and that the focus and attention of the firm on this process would be continuous – in effect, 'business as usual'.

During the embedding sessions, it was explained to participants that the next step would be to run local team or specific practice area sessions where they would have the opportunity to 'deep dive' on individual values and innovate on the delivery of the brand promise. These sessions would not only be led by practice or office heads, but also by other team members keen to take a leadership role in this process.

A microsite was also set up to help track the progress of the team activities and share best practice.

Involvement of: All Bond Dickinson people.

Learning and best practice for embedding a brand within a professional services firm

Learning

Some of the key lessons from this programme were:

- **Client driven.** Brand definition needs to be client driven – bringing client insights to bear is key in achieving engagement and buy in.

- **Clear business rationale.** Provide a clear rationale and business case for the brand – you need to provide the rationale for investment in the brand.

- **Authentic.** The brand and values must feel like an accurate reflection of the firm (and its people) with some stretch to enhance performance.

- **Experiential exercises.** Adopt exercises that raise self-awareness, open minds and deepen the experience to help people move from 'understanding' to 'engagement and commitment'.

- **Not just a strapline.** Brand needs to be seen as more than just a strapline – people in the firm need to understand that brand is as much about 'why we do what we do and what we stand for' as 'what we do'.

- **Leading by example.** When brand and values are driven through the organization by the leaders, far greater commitment is achieved. This process should not be seen as a Marketing or HR initiative.

Best practice

Some of the key points of best practice in executing a programme such as this were:

- **Line of sight.** Critical to show the links and relationship between vision, brand and values.

- **Experience based.** Don't just 'tell and show' – help people *experience* the interdependence between business, brand and culture.

- **Design and adapt.** Prototype, adapt and innovate to ensure the process is compelling and relevant for all audiences within an organization.

- **Leaders involved all the way through.** Ensure leaders own the process, the content and delivery (leaders experience first-hand, and are trained to facilitate and then lead the staff sessions).

- **Marketing and HR experience and resource are very important.** To provide expertise around quality of design, content, framework and logistics, and provide support to leaders throughout process.

Summary

The Bond Dickinson rebranding project could have been no more than a simple renaming of two merged firms. In fact, it became one of the most successful 'inside out' brand programmes in which I have personally been involved.

Why? Because it launched an entirely new firm, with a compelling vision, strategy and brand position; a new firm with a culture designed to support its people in the delivery of that vision.

But the success of the project and indeed the future success of the firm are defined by one thing – the awareness, courage and determination of the leadership team in making it happen.

Internal branding: A roadmap to brand value co-creation

05

FATHIMA SALEEM AND ORIOL IGLESIAS

> **Natalie:** *I purchased the sensitive diapers for new-borns and my baby already has a crazy diaper rash within 2 days of using these diapers!! I have 2 months' worth of diapers that I cannot use now, and a very unhappy baby! I do not recommend these diapers to any new parent* ☹.
>
> **Employee:** [Brand name removed] *sensitive diapers are the best available on the market for new-borns with skin conditions. These diapers meet multiple quality standards and are free of harsh chemicals, chlorine, latex, and fragrance.*

This Facebook conversation was posted on a diaper brand page with over six million followers. The brand is a household name and customer-facing employees are trained to deliver the brand promise and to convert new mothers and fathers into customers by communicating the benefits of the diaper. Although employees are trying to convince parents about the benefits of the diaper through a traditional persuasive approach, it doesn't read like a real dialogue. Consequently, it seems unlikely that Natalie and other new parents would be persuaded by the company's response. The consumer's problem has not been addressed, but rather the employee has taken a defensive and trained stance towards protecting the brand, without creating any value for the customer or relieving the customer's concern about having two months' worth of unusable diapers and an unhappy baby. In the long run, this approach loses the company a considerable amount of customer lifetime value – an American baby needs an average of 4,000 diapers before being toilet trained (Bungert and Darnary, 2008).

Decades ago, the disposable diaper brand would not have had to deal with disgruntled parents on an open social media platform and the interaction with the customer would have been limited to a salesperson in the shop or to a call centre. In these contexts, the company had a high degree of control over its brand. However, with the proliferation of the internet and the wide penetration of social media, various employees can now interact with multitudes of well-informed stakeholders, including customers, potential customers, consumer protection agencies, green groups, and the government. To add further complexity, these conversations are now public and visible to everyone. This is a more transparent and risky environment where brand meaning is no longer determined and enacted solely by the brand, but is co-created among multiple groups of employees and stakeholders, and between stakeholders too. This presents a complex terrain for brands that need to build the necessary tools for their employees to facilitate positive brand value co-creation, rather than taking a controlled approach of simply delivering the brand promise (Iglesias *et al.*, 2013).

Brands operate in a hyper-connected world, in which employees and stakeholders can interact over multiple platforms. Employees who do not have the tools and the skills to navigate these interactions with a variety of stakeholders will be less efficient and successful in co-creating brand value with stakeholders. This highlights the growing importance of internal branding and the need for brands to invest in this area.

Defining internal branding

Even if there is a growing recognition of the key role of internal branding, this is still an emerging field of study, and therefore the field is fuzzy with multiple understandings and definitions of the concept. This is problematic and raises challenges regarding how to better understand and manage internal branding. Saleem and Iglesias

(2016) conducted a systematic literature review of this area to better understand the domain of internal branding, map the field, and provide a more comprehensive definition.

Based on this literature review it is proposed that:

> internal branding is the process through which organizations make a company-wide effort within a supportive culture to integrate brand ideologies, leadership, human resource management, internal brand communications, and internal brand communities as a strategy to enable employees to consistently co-create brand value with multiple stakeholders (Saleem and Iglesias, 2016, p. 50).

Figure 5.1 amalgamates current research to outline a comprehensive understanding of internal branding, which can be applied by brands. However, the components of internal branding are highly interrelated.

Figure 5.1   Framework showing the components of internal branding encapsulated in a supportive corporate culture and the interaction of internal and external stakeholders in co-creating brand value

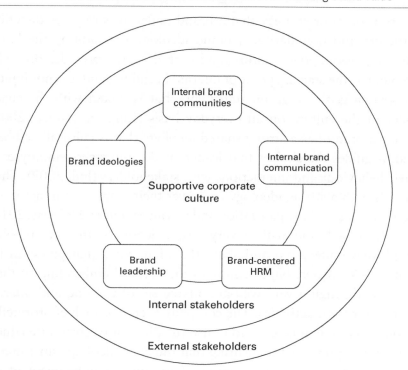

SOURCE Adapted from Saleem and Iglesias (2016)

For example, a clear brand ideology is only possible with the involvement of strong brand leaders who encourage the sharing and implementation of the brand's values. Moreover, internal brand communities (when implemented strategically) can provide an unparalleled platform for various types of internal and external brand communication. The existence of these components leads to a process whereby employees and stakeholders are provided with the necessary tools to co-create brand value, rather than take a rigid approach to 'delivering the brand promise' as illustrated in the story at the beginning of the chapter.

The following sub-sections of this chapter reveal the components of internal branding and explain how organizations implement the various components. The implementation of these components presents a roadmap to facilitate brand value co-creation; however, at the most basic level, internal branding can only thrive in a corporate culture that supports the process.

Brand ideology

Every process or strategy that a brand undertakes requires direction, structure and boundaries. A brand ideology, constituting the brand mission, vision, goals, culture, and shared values, provides this. This ideology is the starting point of internal branding, and it is not limited to written goals or vision statements, but is linked with the enactment of the culture on an everyday basis (King and Grace, 2008). When a brand has a strong shared ideology that is culturally embedded, it guides the choices that leaders make and steers employees in their behaviour and interactions with stakeholders (Ind, 2007). Thus, brands with a strong ideology empower their employees to act in the best interests of the organization and its values (Ind and Iglesias, 2016).

Nike is a brand with a very strong ideology. In fact, all Nike employees understand and share the 11 maxims that guide all the company's actions. Nike reinforces the cultural embedding of these maxims through a very well-articulated set of training and internal communication activities. The company even has a Chief Storyteller, a long-serving employee who is also the director of corporate education and responsible for ensuring that the Nike ideology impregnates every member of the organization. This cultural embedment of the ideology allows Nike to build a very cohesive organization and provide all employees with a good understanding of what the brand stands for and how they should take this into account in their work. Thus, Nike uses storytelling and training to align its employees with the brand ideology and ensure that this ideology is then reflected in everything they do and in the experience they offer customers and other stakeholders. Finally, this strong ideology also facilitates the strategic alignment of all the business units.

In a similar vein, the Ritz Carlton is another corporate brand that puts great effort into ensuring that all employees understand its brand ideology, what it means, and how they should act. Every employee carries a card that contains the guiding principles, or 'credo' of the brand. And, more importantly, every morning they have short meetings called 'daily line-ups', where employees discuss the brand ideology and share stories about the great service delivered by Ritz Carlton employees who acted in accordance with the brand values. The company argues that the daily line-up is an opportunity to reconnect each employee with the purpose and mission of the Ritz Carlton before they start their day.

Finally, brands with a strong ideology are usually perceived as authentic (Beverland, 2005) and generate a strong sense of commitment among stakeholders. Crossfit, a gym franchise with an almost religious following, centres its brand on a military-like, bare-bones competitive workout with a strong sense of community. The focus on good relationships with 'Cross-fitters' is an integral part of the brand ideology that has helped the brand grow quickly (Zmuda, 2011). Thus, a strong and clear brand ideology provides a source of identification and commitment for all members who constitute the brand, ranging from coaches, trainers and corporate personnel to customers. It demonstrates that the components of internal branding can transcend the traditional boundaries of the firm and brand stakeholders.

Brand leadership

If brands are no longer controlled by the organization and are built through a process of collaboration and co-creation with internal and external stakeholders, then we probably need a new type of leadership style that differs from the traditional, authoritative, and top-down approach. This also means that employees are no longer the passive executioners of a corporate script. They become active participants in this ecosystem where brand value is co-created together with customers and other external stakeholders. The key implication is that leaders need to 'stop asking how you can get your employees behind the brand and start thinking about how you can put the brand behind your employees' (Hatch and Schultz, 2008). This requires a new participatory leadership style that should be more empathetic, open and humble – and that also recognizes the need for active employee empowerment (Ind *et al.*, 2013).

Nordstrom, the Seattle-based retailer, is an interesting example because it is known for extraordinary service levels and a highly decentralized leadership and organizational structure. As an illustration of this, the Nordstrom employee handbook is just a postcard that says on one side: 'Our number one goal is to provide outstanding service … our employee handbook is very simple. We only have one rule…' When you turn the card you can read the words: 'Use good judgment in all situations'. This implies that the company trusts its employees, but also that they have been actively trained to understand the brand ideology and how to act accordingly. The key challenge for leaders is to ensure that employees understand and share the brand ideology, and are then set free, as much as possible, to deliver value. Similarly, the social psychologist Michael O'Malley, in his inspiring book *The Wisdom of Bees* (2010), claims that managers should learn from bees. This is because bees have a highly decentralized form of leadership and government that allows the workers who are closest to the information to act upon it immediately and make the most informed decisions.

This new approach to leadership also demands courage and perseverance. Senior managers need to challenge conventions and move the organization in a new direction in accordance with its brand ideology (Iglesias and Bonet, 2010). Paul Polman, the CEO of Unilever, personifies this approach. Under his auspices, Unilever has embarked on 'Sustainable Living Plan' – a strategic plan that aims to double the business size while halving environmental impact by 2020. To follow this plan, Polman had to align all the employees, but possibly even more importantly, he had to challenge the traditional mindset of many of the company's investors and shareholders, who wanted short-term profit. However, the new approach led by the Unilever CEO implies a much longer-term view on the return on investment – as well as the will to make a positive transformational impact on the world that transcends purely economic objectives.

This participative, courageous, and transformative leadership style reduces employee turnover, increases employee commitment, and promotes employee brand building behaviour (on and off the job) through acts such as positive word of mouth to external stakeholders (Morhart *et al.*, 2009). As Zhang *et al.* (2015) suggest, leadership styles that treat internal stakeholders fairly and consistently affect the overall performance of the firm.

Brand-centred human resource management

It is important for internal stakeholders to co-create positive brand value with external stakeholders (including brand partners, employees, and the government) and it is equally important for the structure, policies, and practices of an organization to create positive brand value for potential and existing employees. These structures, policies, and practices constitute the human resource management (HRM) efforts of a company (Iglesias and Saleem, 2015).

Brand-centred HRM starts from the moment of recruiting individuals whose values are congruent with the brand ideology. Think about Disney. Cast members (which is what Disney calls its employees) are not just hired for a job, but to play a role in Disney's show. Every single aspect of Disney's recruiting process is designed to assess the fit of the potential cast member with the Disney brand ideology and culture. During selection interviews, the recruiters look at the education and expertise of candidates, but mainly for a cultural fit and the right attitudes for performing in accordance with the Disney ideology. Disney first hires for culture and attitudes – and then trains the selected cast members (Jones, nd).

When brands consistently train their employees, they provide the opportunity to internalize the brand ideology and act accordingly. Disney trains all its cast members in the same way and independently of their specific job. Each new recruit goes through a training called 'Disney Traditions' that is taught by role model cast members who introduce the new recruits into the Disney culture and spirit of excellence. This is a special characteristic of the Disney training system. Trainers are usually cast members, rather than professional trainers, who know the company from the inside and can share experience and expertise with the rest of the cast. Finally, Disney also has local training sites, called Centres for Excellence, where cast members can learn different job skills and develop new capabilities.

However, under this organic and co-created view of the brand, it is also very important to provide a degree of flexibility to employees so that they can freely decide which skills they want to develop and which topics they want to explore further. In this respect, adidas is another interesting example. The company has moved from a traditional classroom-based approach to a more collaborative and social learning model. In this new model, employees choose what they want to study and learn from experts – as well as peers.

Another two central pieces of brand-centred HRM are promotion and compensation policies and practices. It is essential that the organization recognizes its most talented employees and provides them with the opportunity to grow, while at the same time aligning economic incentives with the desired behaviours that are in tune with the brand ideology.

Internal brand communications

Companies often struggle with establishing and maintaining effective company-wide communication channels; however, internal communication, particularly that which is geared towards facilitating the co-creation of brand value, is important in a company's short- and long-term success. Finnish telecommunications company Nokia was the leader in its industry in another era, but the failure of its mobile devices is partially attributed to issues of internal communications (Groysberg and Slind, 2012). Multiple examples exist of companies that have faced crises or complete failure due to a lack of internal communication, and research suggests that this is one of the crucial contributors towards internal branding (Du Preez and Bendixen, 2015).

Internal brand communication can be separated into four over-arching areas:

1 formal internal communication, for example memos sent by departments;

2 informal internal communications, such as online and offline inter-action with co-workers;

3 formal external communications, such as public relations and advertising; and

4 informal external communications, such as interacting with stake-holders on social media platforms and customer feedback (Miles and Mangold, 2005).

Moving beyond communication that is restricted to within the organization, internal brand communication also constitutes communication with external stakeholders. In a connected world, employees often gain information from stakeholders that can, in turn, influence the identification of the employee with the brand. A concern that brands face is the misalignment between communication that is internal, for instance a highly formalized and top-down internal communication channel, and a formal external communication that is distinct. For example, a brand can promote itself as being highly flexible, hip, and outgoing to customers, while at the same time having a rigid and formal internal communications channel that is entirely inflexible, thus contradicting the marketing image that the company is trying to achieve. Brands with strong internal processes provide employees with the tools to navigate the misaligned internal and external communication (Kapferer, 2012). However, in successfully implementing an internal branding process, all four areas of communication need to operate in unison.

When conducting internal communications, brands also need to understand the current context: the desires and lifestyles of new generations, as well as the hyper-connected and social environment in which we live. Recently, adidas used an engagement survey to ask its employees: 'Do we listen?' The results were interesting. Employees basically replied: 'you're hearing us – but not listening' and 'we feel some degree of remoteness and disconnection with our company' (Synergy, 2017). As a response, adidas intensified its internal communications and put together an ambitious programme of periodic internal conferences, e-mail bulletins, videos, and personalized letters. However, the results were far below management expectations. To discover the reasons, the company conducted qualitative research and found that most of its workforce was already Generation Y. These individuals do not want the company to just talk to them. They want a true dialogue and an inspiring social conversation in which everybody can contribute. They want to engage in social media conversations, they want to know relevant stories about the brand, and they want to give their opinions. adidas has already decided to launch a pilot app that can be personalized and updated regularly, where success and stories can be shared, employee opinions can be listened to, and conversations can be held.

Internal brand communities

The identification of internal brand communities as a component of internal branding is more recent, yet brand communities have had a strong influence on the brand-building process (Veloutsou and Moutinho, 2009). Brands have actively or passively fostered the creation of brand communities that consist of consumers with shared values, beliefs, and interests (Muniz and O'Guinn, 2001). Such communities include the consumers who aggregate around influential YouTube 'make-up gurus' (Singh, 2012), or the AFOLS (Adult Fans of Lego).

In a similar vein, internal brand communities are communities consisting of employees who work for a brand. These communities can exist online or offline (Hatch and Schultz, 2010). The existence of internal brand communities, particularly in global organizations with employees dispersed around the globe, can facilitate employee identification with the brand, create more effective cooperation, and foster employee socialization (Devasagayam *et al.*, 2010; Nambisan and Nambisan, 2008).

With the blurring of boundaries between organizations and stakeholders, internal brand communities can often be open to external stakeholders. For example, the community of Harley Davidson riders includes loyal and passionate consumers who respect and value the brand ethos, as well as employees of the brand (Fournier and Lee, 2009). Brands also draw on communities of employees and external stakeholders for crowdsourcing new product and marketing ideas. Lego's *Idea* site enables stakeholders to contribute ideas for new Lego products, for which support must be garnered from staff and other interested stakeholders. The site involves both internal and external stakeholders for strategic purposes – while at the same time inviting external stakeholders to create brand value.

Opening an organization up to the outside is not always easy. First, many organizations believe that knowledge and expertise is inside and that customers are incapable of bringing relevant contributions to, for instance, an innovation process. Second, many organizations are afraid of the risks of sharing relevant internal information with outsiders. Third, some employees might feel threatened if outsiders bring substantial value to the inside. It is clear that despite these false assumptions and fears, outsiders are capable of bringing valuable ideas and solutions to the inside – as well as effectively collaborating with brand employees. As an example, some years ago NASA was confounded by the challenge of predicting solar flares, which pose a significant radiation risk for equipment and people. As NASA was incapable of achieving accurate results, it launched a crowdsourcing initiative, using the *InnoCentive* site, to see if a more accurate measurement system could be found. Surprisingly, within a few months, a retired radio frequency engineer recorded a 75 per cent accuracy rate, which was much better than the results obtained by NASA. This successful case enlightened NASA about the need to be open and develop collaborative innovation projects with stakeholders.

Outcomes of internal branding

The attitudinal and behavioural outcomes of the process of internal branding can be viewed as a tiered effect. The overall objective of internal branding is to facilitate value co-creation between and among multiple stakeholders. However, in the process of achieving that objective, brands typically aim for specific attitudinal and behavioural outcomes that will foster positive brand value co-creation (Saleem and Iglesias, 2016). However, a rigid internal branding structure can result in simple employee compliance (Morhart *et al.*, 2009), which is a basic and limited initial outcome.

A more relevant attitudinal outcome of internal branding is employee identification with the brand and psychological brand membership. Brand identification is a desired outcome, and may foster other positive behavioural and attitudinal outcomes, such as employee brand commitment. All brands need employees who understand and identify with the brand ideology and values. This is why Disney's recruitment process initially tries to assess if a potential cast member fits with Disney values and culture – and then selected cast members are taught the Disney philosophy and way of doing things. Employee identification is especially important when brands expand and grow in different countries. It is then essential that they all share the core meanings that define the organizational identity – although some cultural differences may remain among employees.

The next attitudinal outcome that internal branding can facilitate is employee brand commitment, which refers to the degree of attachment that employees have towards the brand; this in turn increases an employee's willingness to achieve brand goals. When brands have committed employees, they are ready to go the extra mile. This is especially important in service settings where there are multiple touch points and interactions between brand employees and customers, and where it is difficult to standardize the experience offered. In a study we made in the hospitality industry some years ago (Iglesias *et al.* 2011) we observed that brands with the highest customer satisfaction indexes, capable of building long-term relationships with customers, were those that had extremely committed employees. This commitment was a result of internal branding efforts. Committed employees are empowered to take the necessary action to resolve any potential customer demand and are willing to share their learning and experience with their colleagues, thus facilitating the diffusion of best practices and helping the organization to develop its employees. Disney makes use of these very committed employees to train new cast members. This is the best way that Disney has found to embed new cast members with the Disney ideology and build employee commitment.

A final higher-level attitudinal and behavioural outcome associated with strong and effective internal branding processes is brand

Figure 5.2 Attitudinal and behavioural outcomes of internal branding efforts

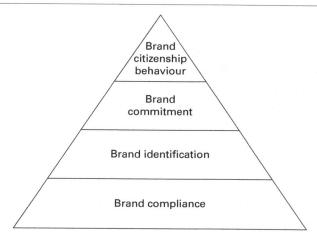

citizenship (Burmann and Zeplin, 2005). This is employee behaviour that goes above and beyond what the company requires from an employee, and can have a very positive impact on other internal and external stakeholders. For example, a cast member at Disney who loves the brand might leave a positive comment about Disney on a website or on Twitter. The employee might also refer the brand to friends and family, and such behaviour would positively impact other employees. The act of leaving a positive comment about Disney on Facebook or Twitter, or recommending the brand to friends, transcends the behaviour that is often required from or expected of employees. This outcome is difficult to achieve but can lead to highly positive brand value co-creation.

Figure 5.2 summarizes the attitudinal and behavioural outcomes of internal branding processes, from simple brand compliance to a more ideal brand citizenship behaviour. Different levels of internal branding can foster different outcomes.

Conclusion

The idea that a brand is a portfolio of meanings, co-created by multiple stakeholders through accumulated interactions, is a significant shift that raises many relevant implications for managers.

First, the brand serves as an interface between customers and employees, but also between employees and other stakeholders. Thus, under this emerging perspective, the organization becomes the brand (Curtis *et al*. 2009). This is because employees can make or break the brand in every single interaction that they have with customers and other stakeholders.

Second, brand management must necessarily place greater emphasis on many other activities in addition to those that have traditionally been core – such as communication or advertising. Building a brand depends on fulfilling promises and offering consistent brand experiences across the various points of contact with stakeholders. This demands the development of a strong internal focus.

Third, the final perceptions of consumers about brands are heavily influenced by the opinions of different stakeholders (outside the organization domain) that use social media as a platform to share their personal experiences with brands. This represents a clear process of power transfer from organizations to such brand communities. The participants in these communities also want to engage in a true dialogue with brands. This means that brand employees cannot simply try to persuade people through scripted interactions on online platforms. They also need to be empowered to listen, to react and to engage in an authentic conversation.

All in all, internal branding is key to building strong and enduring brands. It is a company-wide effort that within a supportive culture needs to integrate brand ideologies, leadership, human resource management, internal brand communications, and internal brand communities as a strategy to enable employees to consistently co-create brand value with multiple stakeholders.

References

Beverland, M (2005) Brand management and the challenge of authenticity, *Journal of Product & Brand Management*, **14** (7), pp. 460–61

Burmann, C and Zeplin, S (2005) Building brand commitment: A behavioural approach to internal brand management, *Journal of Brand Management*, **12** (4), pp. 279–300

Bungert, P J and Darnay, A J (eds.) (2008) *Encyclopedia of Products & Industries – Manufacturing Vol. 1*, Detroit: Gale, pp. 363–71

Curtis, T, Abratt, R and Minor, W (2009) Corporate brand management in higher education: The case of ERAU, *Journal of Product & Brand Management*, **18** (6), pp. 404–13

Du Preez, R, and Bendixen, M T (2015) The impact of internal brand management on employee job satisfaction, brand commitment and intention to stay, *International Journal of Bank Marketing*, **33** (1), pp. 78–91

Fournier, S and Lee, L (2009) Getting brand communities right, *Harvard Business Review*, **87** (4), pp. 105–11

Groysberg, B and Slind, M (2012) The silent killer of big companies, *Harvard Business Review*, October

Hatch, M J and Schultz, M (2008) *Taking Brand Initiative: How companies can align strategy, culture and identity through corporate branding*, San Francisco: Jossey-Bass, p. 17

Hatch, M J and Schultz, M (2010) Toward a theory of brand co-creation with implications for brand governance, *Journal of Brand Management*, **17** (8), pp. 590–604

Iglesias, O and Bonet, E (2010) Persuasive brand management: How managers can influence brand meaning when they are losing control over it, *Journal of Organizational Change Management*, **25** (2), pp. 251–64

Iglesias, O, Ind, N and Alfaro, M (2013) The organic view of the brand: A brand value co-creation model, *Journal of Brand Management*, **20** (8), pp. 670–88

Iglesias, O and Saleem, F Z (2015) How to support consumer-brand relationships: The role of corporate culture and human resource policies and practices, *Marketing Intelligence & Planning*, **33** (2), pp. 216–34

Iglesias, O, Sauquet, A and Montaña, J (2011) The role of corporate culture in relationship marketing, *European Journal of Marketing*, **45** (4), pp. 631–50

Ind, N (2007) *Living the Brand: How to transform every member of your organization into a brand champion*, London: Kogan Page

Ind, N and Iglesias, O (2016) *Brand desire: How to create consumer involvement and inspiration*, London: Bloomsbury

Ind, N, Iglesias, O and Schultz, M (2013) Building brand together: Emergence and outcomes of co-creation, *California Management Review*, **55** (3), pp. 5–26

Jones, B I (nd) People management lessons from Disney, *Disney Institute* [online] https://cdns3.trainingindustry.com/media/3532077/disneypeoplemanagementlessons.pdf [accessed November 2016]

Kapferer, J N (2012) *The New Strategic Brand Management: Advanced insights and strategic thinking*, London: Kogan Page

King, C and Grace, D (2008) Internal branding: Exploring the employee's perspective, *Journal of Brand Management*, **15** (5), pp. 358–72

Miles, S J and Mangold, W G (2005) Positioning Southwest Airlines through employee branding, *Business Horizons*, **48** (6), pp. 535–45

Morhart, F M, Herzog, W and Tomczak, T (2009) Brand-specific leadership: Turning employees into brand champions, *Journal of Marketing*, **73** (5), pp. 122–42

Muniz, A M and O'Guinn, T C (2001) Brand community, *Journal of Consumer Research*, **27** (4), pp. 412–32

Nambisan, S and Nambisan, P (2008) How to profit from a better 'virtual customer environment', *MIT Sloan Management Review*, **49** (3), p. 53

O'Malley, M (2010) *The Wisdom of Bees: What the hive can teach business about leadership, efficiency, and growth*, Viking Books

Raj Devasagayam, P, Buff, C L, Aurand, T W and Judson, K M (2010) Building brand community membership within organizations: A viable internal branding alternative? *Journal of Product & Brand Management*, **19** (3), pp. 210–17

Saleem, F Z and Iglesias, O (2016) Mapping the domain of the fragmented field of internal branding, *Journal of Product & Brand Management*, **25** (1), pp. 43–57

Singh, S (2012). The JC Penney Company and Sephora USA partnership: A case study, *Journal of Business Case Studies*, **8** (6), p. 609

Synergy (2017) The BOC Internal Communications Conference, *Synergy* [online] http://www.synergycreative.co.uk/images/Download_documents/Synergy_notes_Internal_Comms_Conference.pdf [accessed 15 February 2017]

Veloutsou, C and Moutinho, L (2009) Brand relationships through brand reputation and brand tribalism, *Journal of Business Research*, **62** (3), pp. 314–22

Zhang, X A, Li, N, Ullrich, J and van Dick, R (2015) Getting everyone on board the effect of differentiated transformational leadership by CEOs on top management team effectiveness and leader-rated firm performance, *Journal of Management*, **41** (7), pp. 1898–1933

Zmuda, N (2011) America's hottest brands, *Advertising Age*, **82** (42), p. 44

Transforming brand and culture at NN Group

06

Involving employees in an international insurance company to actively develop and foster a more personal and caring brand and culture

MARIJE SCHOLMA, REMCO BARBIER AND CHRIS KERSBERGEN

> Following the divestment from ING in the aftermath of the financial crisis, NN Group's journey towards becoming a stand-alone company involved many exciting and challenging steps. Working from operational separation towards an Initial Public Offering (IPO), the biggest challenge was to rebuild the brand, the culture, and the identity for the company – a process in which the active inclusion of managers and employees was crucial.

The beginning

NN Group was listed on the Euronext stock exchange in Amsterdam on 2 July 2014. It was the closing piece of five years of restructuring, strategy development and brand building. NN Group is a Netherlands-based financial services group, encompassing NN, Nationale-Nederlanden and NN Investment Partners. Following the IPO, the NN brand's, purpose and values were rolled out in every country where NN group is active. Today, NN Group is a rebranded, stand-alone company with around 11,500 employees in 18 countries.

The success of NN Group's rebranding was not only due to the practical rebranding process and necessary organizational changes, but even more because it went hand in hand with a cultural shift. It was an example of creativity, collaboration, inclusion and rigorous execution at all levels of the organization.

The development of a new brand

It's fair to say that NN Group's brand journey hasn't been an easy one to navigate. In a period of uncertainty in the financial sector and lack of clarity of the future for the company it was a challenge to plan, which took its toll on those involved, affecting their engagement, pride and confidence. This is why we had to ensure that during the brand development process, broad groups of managers and employees from every country and business line were involved. And as for a time we didn't have an agreed brand name to work with, an interim internal brand was introduced, called 'FWD' (*forward*).

The brand development process started with looking externally – surveying more than 20,000 consumers, generating customer feedback and talking to business partners. The consumer research focused on the underlying emotions consumers have regarding their financial futures. It showed that consumers appeared insecure, confused and uncertain about their future financial planning. They were looking for intuitive, personal ways to deal with their financial matters by addressing those aspects of their life that were most important to them.

Equally important to the external consumer insights was to make sure business leaders from the 18 countries in which NN Group operates were involved in a rigorous brand and strategy creation process. And not only senior leaders were involved – all employees were invited using different tools to participate in the brand- and strategy-creating process.

'FWD Dialogue': a global webchat involving more than 400 employees in a strategy dialogue

Leadership conferences are crucial events to engage and align our top people in evolving the strategic direction of the company. The events are typically attended by between 50 and 200 of the most senior leaders. At one of these conferences the organizing team was keen to include a broader group of managers and employees in a dialogue around key strategic themes. From the conference location, a 'webchat' with different chatrooms based on strategic topics was set up, allowing every employee to participate from a distance.

The global scope, combined with the dependency on external IT infrastructures, made this quite a risky enterprise. But the internal communications team was confident enough to go through with the event. Over 400 employees representing all the countries where we operate joined the 'FWD Dialogue' platform and chatted directly with the leaders gathered at the event.

The FWD Dialogue generated a wealth of input and feedback on the key strategic themes, as well as a sense of inclusion. The direct contact and the personal commitment of the senior leaders were greatly appreciated.

Ultimately, 300 possible options for the brand name were explored in 19 languages and 23 dialects. From the results of the internal and external research, the brand NN was chosen – balancing NN's Dutch roots and 170-year-old heritage with the requirements of an international and future-proof brand. Building on the outcomes of both the branding and strategy process, the new purpose became 'We secure people's financial futures'.

The slogan for the new international brand campaign became 'You matter', representing NN Group's ambition to become the most human, relatable brand in long-term financial planning. NN aims to be a brand that is genuinely interested in things that matter to people beyond merely finance and insurance – 'what matters to them, matters to us'. NN wants to inspire people to think about what matters most to them, and encourage and support them to take real action towards realizing and protecting their personal goals and dreams.

The new values: care, clear, commit

Building on the outcomes of the international branding research as well as the employee input from the FWD Workshops, corporate communications, human resources, legal and compliance and business leaders worked together to formulate the new company values.

Supporting the brand, purpose and culture of the company, the new values became:

- CARE. We empower people to be their best and respect each other and the world we live in.
- CLEAR. We communicate proactively and honestly, while being accessible and open.
- COMMIT. We act with integrity and do business with the future in mind.

Choosing human, relatable values and choosing them as the only values for the company was a conscious decision, and one that led to quick familiarity with the values amongst NN Group colleagues – one year after their introduction, internal research showed a 91 per cent overall recognition of the values.

The values, written down in the NN Statement of Living our Values, are not voluntary suggestions; they apply to each and every employee. They are the foundation of the company culture and guide our employees in their day-to-day interactions with different stakeholder groups.

'FWD Workshops': using gaming mechanics to build the brand together

The preliminary brand and brand values were tested and sharpened in different rounds through 'FWD Workshops' in every country. Each country received a video from the CEO with an interactive, online game soliciting their feedback on the preliminary contours of the brand positioning and values. Around 750 managers in 20 countries actively participated in two different modules. The first one concerned the envisioned customer experience, and the second focused on the required culture.

The online platform automatically aggregated all the feedback from the countries back to the participants and to the central team. This offered the central team valuable insight into the meaning and associations around the aspired brand values and culture. This direct involvement of managers from every country made a significant contribution to the progress and buy-in for the further development process of the brand.

Internal branding: 'you matter begins with you...'

Before the official rebranding process started, leaders and employees across the company were introduced to the new values and brand under the umbrella 'You matter starts with you...' Several introduction campaigns and events took place at both head office and within the business units.

It was also a top priority to engage all employees in the lead-up to the IPO, as well as on the day itself; NN Group was determined to create a relevant, fun and unifying event from this significant milestone.

The IPO was also the first time the NN brand was actively communicated externally, showcasing a new logo and a visual identity that was designed to combine clarity and warmth. The corporate IPO campaign literally showed a human face by featuring real NN employees. And on the day itself, NN's board members arrived by bicycle to the Amsterdam Stock Exchange, which gave the event a personal touch that drew on the company's Dutch roots, and was picked up favourably by the media. An internal social platform was created where employees in all countries could follow a live-stream television show for employees, broadcast from Euronext Amsterdam. NN Group was the first company in the history of the stock exchange to organize such a live event for their employees.

Turning the IPO into an employee engagement and unification event

On 2 July 2014, NN Group was listed on the Euronext Amsterdam Stock Exchange. This was the third-largest Initial Public Offering (IPO) in 20 years in Europe. Externally, a short corporate campaign introduced NN Group to future investors, featuring real employees telling the company story.

The IPO was a major milestone, leaving five years of restructuring behind, and marking a fresh start for NN Group and its 11,500 employees worldwide. Rather than keep the event small and confined to the head office, the communications team created an inclusive, all-employee celebration, using the 'You matter' storyline.

The guiding principles were:

Be open and make it relevant. The IPO was made relevant by communicating and celebrating every single milestone, formal and informal. From the launch of the new website to the publication of the prospectus, each piece of information was made easy to understand and inclusive. In the Dutch home market, tours were organized to the Amsterdam Stock Exchange, where the stock would be listed; almost 1,000 people signed up.

Make it personal and use local language. The 'You matter' brand only becomes reality if NN's employees know what it means and how to contribute to the goal. Implementing this from the beginning, the theme for the IPO was: '*You matter begins with you. Be part of this moment*', with all materials translated into the 12 working languages within NN Group.

Make it fun and easy to participate. Through the #YourNNSelfie selfie competition, party prop kits, local celebrations and video movies made on the fly. #YourNNSelfie was a global 'selfie' contest, kicked off by the CEO, and invited all colleagues worldwide to take a selfie with an 'NN' attribute and to upload these on the social intranet platform. Hundreds of colleagues uploaded their selfies, and the best selfie from each country (decided by the number of likes per picture) won a trip to Amsterdam and a role in the next leadership conference. Countries shared videos and images of their celebrations, contributing to compilations that showed thousands of employees from around the globe celebrating this event in the same spirit.

Give and get. Share the future success of our IPO with a special savings plan. A voluntary employee savings plan called 'ShareSave' was developed, allowing employees to save a fixed amount of money for 36 months, and to receive a gross gain if at the end of this period the NN share prices increased compared to the share price on the first day of listing. Thirty per cent of all colleagues signed up for the programme.

Make it memorable. A unique event celebrated at the exact same time and special NN-branded gifts to capture the moment. NN Group was the first company to broadcast live from Euronext, with a live TV programme streaming to 45 locations in 18 countries around the world, counting down to the moment that the CEO hit the gong.

Involve local communications teams. Getting them committed and sharing a common goal. All celebrations were organized within a timeframe of two weeks and were carried out over solid timelines in close partnership with the local communications teams and CEOs in all the countries.

In the end, the campaigns and celebrations around the IPO day connected 11,500 colleagues in 45 locations in 18 countries around a shared milestone.

The next phase: transforming brand and culture

In addition to introducing the purpose, values and 'You matter' brand essence, many changes were being made to better align NN Group's products, services and processes with the values and brand. The international rebranding operation offered a unique opportunity to critically review and redesign every touch point of the brand with the consumer, from websites and campaigns to brochures and call centre scripts. In one year, more than 500 colleagues worked on the international rebranding programme, over 1,000 IT applications and 350 portals were rebranded, and 7,500 letters were updated in terms of design, fonts and branding.

In addition to external efforts, internally NN Group wanted to keep the momentum of the brand transformation going, while at the same time increasing the connection between the brand, values, and day-to-day jobs. To do so, NN launched the 'Living our Values' programme, focused on making the values a fully integrated part of the culture. One initiative was the NN Values challenge, a serious, online game introduced in 2015 that allowed colleagues to put the NN values into practice and see how their choices directly affect customers. In the game, colleagues competed against each other, making decisions with the values as a guide (throughout NN Group, in their own local language) in scenarios involving different stakeholders.

This serious game was considered a great success, with about 2,000 colleagues engaged in the game and local winners playing final rounds against management board members. Colleagues felt that the NN Values challenge was a fun, interactive way to put the values into practice, while at the same time learning more about international colleagues and local cultures with regards to the values. The NN Values challenge was repeated in 2016 and was also part of broader, yearly NN Values week, which serves to highlight the values by way of events and activities at head office and within the business units.

It's all about people

NN Group recognized that the potential to truly support the 'You matter' brand promise was rooted in the mindset and capabilities of its people.

Taking into account that our customers are emotional beings that make decisions based on intuition, beliefs and trust, NN Group set out to better develop 'right brain' aspects such as creativity and empathy amongst employees, attributes that would complement an industry traditionally managed by logic, analysis and facts. Together, these characteristics would also foster a sense of innovation within NN Group, deemed a key focus area for the company.

Unleashing the full potential of employees also requires a trust-driven, rather than control-driven, organizational culture. Creating the right climate and empowering leaders to improve their leadership skills was also top of the agenda as NN Group moved forward.

In the year following the rebrand, every senior leader followed a new multi-day leadership programme that included topics like business best practice, innovation and strategy deployment, combined with self-awareness and people leadership skills. Each programme was visited by one of the management board members to show their interest and support.

Simultaneously the Performance Management approach was transformed at the senior level. The shift was from a traditional one-to-one that centres around regular performance check-ins throughout the year to focus more on employees' motivation, development and growth.

Aligning the NN Employee Value Proposition

At NN personality matters. We believe that especially in a
dedicated team as ours individual talents and ideas make
a difference. It gives us a unique perspective. A fresh way
to look at problems. And ultimately leads to better results.
Are you ready to step up and take the initiative?

Find out more about our opportunities for
IT-Professional at www.nncareers.com

NN Descriptor You matter

NN Group is well aware that people are our differentiator for long-term
success. How our people approach customers, live our values and brand,
and their behaviours, mindset and attitudes are what make our company
unique. From this, the central message in the employer branding activities
became that 'personality is as important as competence'. After many
sessions with employees from around the company, a new 'Employee
Value Proposition' (EVP) was developed with 'You matter' as the underlying
ideal. The new proposition elaborated how NN Group encourages
employees to express and develop their talents and personalities
through flexible working agreements and direct influence on their own
development, among other opportunities.

Successful employer branding strategies work from the inside out.
This means creating unique, characteristic culture stories and then
communicating them to the right audiences and future talents, while
leveraging the dynamics of today's social media landscape. This has been
the starting point for NN Group's most recent efforts to achieve an employer
of choice position with talent groups that are critical to our future success.

Measuring success: moving in the right direction

NN Group's efforts to be a company that really matters in the lives of all stakeholders is something that will prove its success over time. Measurements show the company is moving in the right direction.

To date, employee engagement has risen to a steady 86 per cent, a significant increase compared to the year before the rebrand. In addition, a result from the same survey showed that 86 per cent of employees provided positive feedback on their perceptions of how NN is living its values and brand.

To monitor how the NN brand is perceived externally amongst customers and society at large, the NN Global Brand Health Monitor was developed in 2015. It is a core evaluation of the health of the NN brand. Twice a year, the main brand indicators are measured and insight is provided in the development of brand performance.

The Global Brand Health Monitor measures the brand awareness per business line per country, and whether customers feel NN is living its values. It also measures the so-called Relationship Net Promoter Score (NPS), which we believe is an important measure for brand preference and performance.

Since rebranding from ING to NN in the first half year of 2015, the majority of NN's insurance businesses have restored the aided brand awareness levels and maintained or improved their Relationship NPS scores; in most cases, NN scores on or above the market average. In nine insurance countries, a growing number of people recognize NN as the 'You matter' company.

Going forward: You matter 2.0

A brand needs maintenance, and needs to develop with the external world. NN Group wants to be known as the 'You matter' company: a people-oriented and authentic service provider in the long-term financial planning industry. 'You matter' is not just a slogan; it defines what is done at NN, influencing every department, every employee and every interaction with customers.

Also, going forward, with 'You matter', NN wants to inspire people to think about what matters most to them, and to instil in them the confidence and wisdom to secure their financial futures. This also means that NN takes an active role in helping customers recognize what truly matters to them in life. NN's campaigns, focused on understanding the deeper motivations of individuals, and sharing what makes our customers happy, play an important role in this.

In 2016, a new campaign was launched – 'It's different when it's yours' – celebrating the uniqueness of each individual customer. It focuses on those moments in life we all experience, yet we all experience so differently. So even though NN is proud to help millions of families, homes and businesses every day, they know that the family, home or business of each individual customer will matter most to him or her.

One of the positive aspects from the first 'You matter' campaign was that it enabled business units to choose and edit different scenes, based on their own preferences. This time we wanted to extend this modular approach further: to be even more relevant to different groups of customers and flexible in helping them achieve local marketing objectives while maintaining consistency of brand experience. Therefore, the strategic proposition has been carefully defined in close cooperation with marketing and communication colleagues from the business units.

Practically, we have created much more film footage and material this time, covering subjects that range across relationships, love, homes, families, passion and much more. From the selection of created content, business units can choose those subjects and scenes that are most relevant to their audiences. This focus on relevance has contributed to stronger local identification and employee advocacy around the campaign messages.

We believe it is the appealing combination of the purpose to secure people's financial futures and the values of care, clear, commit, that drives the personal commitment of all NN's employees across every market, as they bring the brand to life, every day.

'Living the CSR brand': Model, best practices and recommendations

07

CARSTEN BAUMGARTH AND LARS BINCKEBANCK

CSR brand without 'living the brand' is dangerous

In contrast to the notion of sustainability, which broadly refers to a general guiding principle for society, Corporate Social Responsibility (CSR) can be defined as a specific firm going beyond legal obligations to consider voluntarily its stakeholders' social, environmental, ethical and human rights concerns both within and outside its business operations (Aguilera *et al.*, 2007; Godfrey *et al.*, 2009; Homburg *et al.*, 2013). Stakeholders can be seen as persons or groups that have any ownership, rights or interests in a firm and its activities, including customers, suppliers, employees, investors and the communities in which they operate (Clarkson, 1995). Scholars and practitioners have found that CSR efforts and communications can enhance stakeholder perceptions (Sen and Bhattacharya, 2001) while a lack thereof might damage stakeholder relationships (Becker-Olsen *et al.*, 2011).

If brand management is a systematic process to create differentiating and preference-inducing associations in the minds of the relevant customers (de Chernatony, 2010), then CSR branding can be defined as a systematic process to create differentiating and preference-inducing, social, ecological, ethical and/or human rights associations in the minds of the relevant stakeholders. CSR branding is, therefore, a special type of brand management distinguished from traditional approaches first through its type of brand values, and second through its broad coverage of stakeholder groups.

However, CSR branding 'can be a dangerous endeavour' (Vallaster *et al.*, 2012, p. 35). Stakeholders have very different and often contradictory expectations regarding a firm's CSR activities. When claims of CSR as a guiding value system turn out to be window dressing or greenwashing, the violating brand can become a target of increased scrutiny and public outcry and suffer badly as a result, rightfully being accused of hypocrisy and deceiving the public (Palazzo and Basu, 2007). Thus, a CSR brand must be intrinsically based on a credible and authentic CSR-related brand value core that connects with relevant stakeholder groups. While a more traditional brand can be defined by what it does and represents, a CSR brand is also determined by who it is (Vallaster *et al.*, 2012).

According to Hatch and Schultz (2003), the claimed values of the brand must resonate with the tacit meanings and values of the organizational members or, in other words, it must be congruent with the firm's identity, personality and culture. If successful, the brand can establish associations in the minds of stakeholders that can help to differentiate the brand from its competitors (Keller and Richey, 2006). To achieve this, CSR branding must involve the whole company, including employees, in brand delivery (Vallaster *et al.* 2012). The concept of internal brand management is based on the view that the behaviour of employees lies at the heart of any brand, offering a potential route to acquiring sustainable competitive advantage by means of building a strong brand whose positioning is extremely difficult for competitors to imitate. While the contribution of each individual employee may differ in degree and scope, none are negligible when it comes to building a strong brand externally – through 'living it' internally (Burmann *et al.*, 2009).

Employees who are loyal to and 'live' the brand (Ind, 2007) align their personal values with those of the brand, and their behaviour communicates these brand values to internal and external stakeholders (Wallace and de Chernatony, 2008). At a more operational level, employees can enhance customer relationships through their behaviour during interactive encounters, creating a lasting impression of and lending authenticity to the brand on top of increased employee satisfaction and incremental sales (Baumgarth and Binckebanck, 2011).

Gelb and Rangarajan (2014, p. 98) assert that 'employees can "make or break" brands in two related ways'. First, as a touch point for stakeholder interactions, employees are an integral element of any brand. Because human behaviour can only be standardized to a limited degree, it can yield unexpected results. Thus, employees as 'the least standardized aspect of a brand' (Gelb and Rangarajan, 2014, p. 98) are the most likely sources of the most intense brand experiences, be they positive or negative. Second, beyond their specific job description, employees can represent the brand to other stakeholders as brand ambassadors, both internally and externally, thereby tangibly embodying brand values, defending the brand in times of crisis and bringing in feedback from outside sources.

As employee behaviour impacts brand perceptions (such as credibility, authenticity or trust) and ultimately affects the company's bottom line, influencing first employee attitudes and then their behaviour should be an integral part of any branding strategy, in particular for CSR brands that rely on a tight fit between internal values and external communication. A failure to do so might result in damage to the CSR brand if customers or other stakeholders (eg journalists, bloggers, NGOs) find a gap between the communicated CSR-related values and the actual behaviour of employees 'living the brand' and, by extension, the firm, endangering the corporate licence to operate.

This chapter aims to support CSR branding in general and, more specifically, to highlight the respective contributions of employees and their 'living the brand'. In a first step, the big picture of CSR branding is presented from a macro perspective. A holistic CSR brand management model is proposed and illustrated using a best-practice example from Germany. The second step deals with the micro perspective of 'living the brand' by reviewing relevant research and then offering insights through specific best-practice examples on leadership, human resource management and internal communication.

Macro-perspective (big picture) 'living the CSR brand'

CSR brand management model

To design a model for CSR branding, we build on identity-based brand management models. Of these, we have chosen the model by Hatch and Schulz (2001, 2008) which was established and tested for corporate brands, for further development and adaption to the CSR challenge described above. It assumes that a brand is made up of three elements: (1) strategic vision covers the goals and strategic decisions of the top management; (2) business culture describes the shared values of all employees; and (3) image denotes the experiences and expectations of external stakeholders.

According to the model, a strong brand identity results when these three building blocks show a high fit. It also interprets brands as concepts developed internally from the brand identity. However, the model neglects the actual behaviour of the firm and the communication of the brand identity to the various stakeholders. As these two facets are especially important for CSR brands, we have extended the basic model accordingly. Furthermore, the original dimension of strategic vision has been replaced by the concept of brand positioning, denoting a conscious decision about the target status of the brand from the manager's viewpoint. This includes, especially for corporate brands, the vision and mission of the company. Figure 7.1 illustrates the resulting CSR brand management model.

The model incorporates the following five building blocks:

1 **Positioning**. This contains the explicit decision making by the (top) management about the basic orientation of the brand, with the vision and mission of the company as integral components. Descriptive and evaluative features are whether, and to what extent, the brand positioning comprehensively includes CSR, whether this results from altruistic motives in top management, whether the brand positioning is codified in writing, as well as whether this is evaluated as relevant and actively put into practice by top management.

Figure 7.1 Holistic CSR brand model

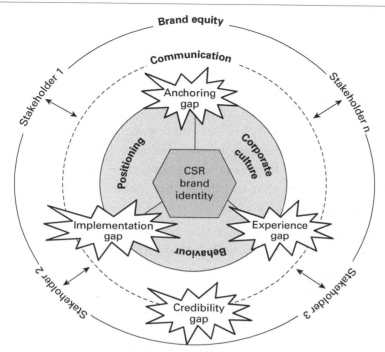

SOURCE Baumgarth/Binckebanck 2015, p. 39

2 Corporate culture. This dimension covers values shared by all employees. In line with the corporate culture model by Schein (1999, 2004), these values can be reflected in explicit and implicit norms and rules (eg corporate governance, guidelines for energy saving) and symbols (eg use of electric company cars, building architecture, workplace design). A CSR brand is based on the perception by all employees of the CSR idea as relevant, leading them to embrace and actively support it. This dimension also includes all management instruments that can be used to establish the CSR brand positioning inside the company.

3 Behaviour. This includes concrete measures by the company that are effective both internally and externally. The degree of CSR implementation into the actual corporate and individual behaviour can be described and evaluated with the help of the value chain, from sourcing and production via distribution through to recycling. It should also be evaluated whether the CSR-relevant measures cover all functional areas and regional locations.

4 **Communication.** This takes into consideration all externally directed personal or media contacts with the various stakeholder groups. From a CSR point of view, credibility is of vital importance. This, in turn, is affected by factors such as transparency, proof-of-claims through verifiable facts (eg CSR reports, certificates, participation in CSR-oriented awards), openness and real interaction with the various stakeholders. Moreover, the actual branding (name, logo, brand colours, etc.) creates the central brand touchpoint that facilitates and enables the perception and experience of the CSR identity.

5 **Gaps.** The fit of the model's facets is very high up on the scale of major success factors for CSR brands. An anchoring gap is present when the orientation of the brand, as propagated and fixed by top management, does not correspond to the convictions and values held and acted upon by the employees. The experience gap results from deviations in the actual behaviour of the company (eg products) and the values shared within the workforce. An implementation gap means that the defined CSR values are not converted into actual behaviour. Finally, a credibility gap can occur when the CSR brand identity and the external communications do not conform. This differentiation along four gaps simplifies and supports the analysis of real CSR brands. In reality, a simultaneous balance between the four facets is called for to create strong CSR brands.

The brand equity at the outside shell of the model is not actually part of the brand management because it is not directly manageable. Instead, brand equity is the final outcome of brand management at the stakeholder level.

Best practice: Werkhaus

Werkhaus is a German company with approximately 150 employees which was founded in 1992 by Holger and Eva Danneberg. It makes products for living and working environments, toys, and displays for retail and exhibitions, all based on wood. Around 70 per cent of turnover today comes from the b-to-b sector.

1 **Positioning.** From the beginning, the following four values were defined as integral brand components: social responsibility, innovative products, high ecological standards and production – 'Made in Germany'. Even though these values were not formulated as part of a brand positioning statement, they are explicitly codified in all print (eg catalogues, advertisements) and other (eg website) communications.

2 **Corporate culture.** The culture is heavily influenced by the political views and earlier activities of the founders, who used to take part in the German civil movement to exit nuclear power. The values are 'lived' in day-to-day routines, and can also be found in symbols. For example, the ecological positioning can be detected not just in the use of wood as the primary raw material for the products, but also in a separate wood-fired power plant, a bio-food canteen, electricity from regenerative sources (Greenpeace Energy) and use of recycled paper in the office and in communications media. As part of their social positioning, employment opportunities are specifically designed for the mentally handicapped or physically disabled, who make up approximately 15 per cent of their workforce (the average in Germany is 3–4 per cent). Moreover, Werkhaus also offers an above-average number of apprenticeships, flexible working hours, equal opportunities, reconciliation of work and family, and bases its production facilities in a structurally weak rural area in Germany. In summary, Werkhaus exhibits a corporate culture that was developed by the founders, that is systematically communicated both internally and externally, and that is generally 'lived' at all levels of the organization. The founders appear to be ready to accept compromises in terms of profitability for the sake of positive mood, satisfaction and a sense of meaning at work for all employees.

3 **Behaviour.** At the core of the business model, the founders' ecological philosophy is translated into the manufacturing of tangible products. The packaging is designed to minimize emissions during transport. There is a strong emphasis on sustainability, from the sourcing of raw materials (eg wood from recycling, innocuous paints) to the reduction, recovery and utilization of waste. For example, employees are systematically trained to avoid waste. The overall ecological standards of WERKHAUS have been recognized with several awards. Social standards in human resource management are also high, from workplaces specifically designed for the

disabled and equal pay for disabled and handicapped employees to value-based recruiting, training and events (eg summer and Christmas parties). In the afternoon or when there is no school, employees can bring their children to work, where they are taken care of in dedicated day care areas.

4 Communication. The branding of Werkhaus (name and logo) has been mostly unaltered since the early days of their inception. Important media for external communication are the website and the online shop. In terms of b-to-b communications, there is an additional emphasis on exhibitions, both national and international. In the b-to-c segment, on the other hand, the annual catalogue, with 15,000 copies printed, plays a vital role in communications. There are also regular advertisements in magazines with a focus on eco and design themes. Since 2009, Werkhaus has begun to open fully owned brand shops. Currently, there are eight of these shops in premium locations that offer and stage the full b-to-c product range.

To summarize, Werkhaus can be described as a 'real' CSR brand (Baumgarth and Binckebanck, 2015) that clearly shows CSR-related attributes on all four facets of the CSR brand management model. During our case study analysis, the framework was found to be highly useful and has proven to be remarkably robust and flexible. It does indeed appear to provide a suitable framework for a comprehensive and detailed analysis of real-life CSR brands. It can, therefore, be assumed that the model might also be useful in a prescriptive way, helping managers striving to build 'real' CSR brands to make better choices. To elaborate on aspects of 'living the brand', the next section of this chapter will adopt a micro perspective and focus in on the specifically related aspects.

Micro-perspective 'living the CSR brand'

Internal CSR brand management and internal CSR brand equity

Brand orientation is an inside-out and identity-driven approach aligning strategy with the brand, which considers the brand as a strategic asset and a source of sustained competitive advantage (Urde *et al.*, 2013). In brand-oriented firms, senior managers accord high relevance to branding (Baumgarth, 2010) and align business with brand strategy, using the brand as a 'beacon' to inspire the employees and allow them to be efficient brand ambassadors, ultimately leading to higher brand equity (Gromark and Melin, 2011). When employees identify with and convey the core values of the organization (Urde, 1999), they 'live the brand' (Ind, 2007), their behaviour reinforces brand identity, and they become a strategic resource for the firm (de Chernatony, 2010).

Thus, a brand-oriented CSR culture can facilitate a shared understanding of CSR-related brand values and acceptance of said values by employees across the organization (Homburg and Pflesser, 2000). Internal brand management, defined as the systematically planned management of behaviour, communication and symbolism to attain a favorable and positive reputation for an organization (Einwiller and Will, 2002) can promote person–organization fit, making employees better brand ambassadors who can effectively deliver values to stakeholders (Matanda and Ndubisi, 2013). Internal CSR branding ensures that all employees understand the objectives, positioning and features of the CSR brand promise. Thus, firms can ensure that the espoused CSR brand values that set stakeholders' expectations are enacted and delivered by employees (Punjaisri and Wilson, 2011).

Burmann and Zeplin (2005) have presented a behavioural model of internal brand management that is based on a brand identity approach. It identifies the establishment of employees' brand commitment and brand citizenship behaviour as the pivotal constituents for successful internal brand management and, in turn, brand strength. Brand commitment refers to the extent of psychological attachment of employees to the brand, which influences their willingness to exert extra effort toward reaching the brand's goals, that is, to exhibit brand citizenship behaviour that enhances brand identity. Brand commitment was found to be the result of three determinants, namely brand-centered human resources management, brand communication, and brand leadership (Burmann *et al.*, 2009).

To ensure that employees are 'living the CSR brand,' it is thus necessary to implement an internal CSR brand management that systematically employs leadership by persons and systems, human resources management and internal communications to drive employee commitment to the CSR brand with positive effects on their brand-related behaviour and, ultimately, CSR brand equity. In the following section, best practices from CSR brands in Germany will be used to shed light on the three determinants of CSR brand commitment.

Success factors and best practices

Leadership by persons and systems

A first pillar of the internal CSR brand management is leadership. The literature on internal and CSR brand management emphasizes the relevance of top management for the enhancement of internal brand equity. Some papers mention the role of leadership in general (eg Bernal, 2016; Burmann and Zeplin, 2005; Miles and Mangold, 2004; Vallaster and de Chernatony, 2006), whereas other papers analyse individual facets, like leadership style (eg Morhart *et al.*, 2009), the role of the founder (Hillestad *et al.*, 2010), type of motivation of the top management (eg Angus-Leppan *et al.*, 2010; Ellen *et al.*, 2006), and explicit or implicit rules (eg Baumgarth, 2010).

On an abstract level, leadership can be divided into two interrelated fields, namely the leader (ie personality, leadership style) and leadership instruments. For both categories, a list of success factors can be formulated as follows.

1 Altruistic, ethical and value-driven motivation An authentic and trustworthy CSR brand is based on values and an inside-out perspective. That means that the founders and/or the top management act because of an intrinsic motivation and upon a CSR-oriented value set. Top management's decisions are not merely a reaction to influences from NGOs or other external stakeholders, but are rather based on personal and deep beliefs. An ethical leader demonstrates a sense of right and wrong, concern for others inside and outside the company, and a willingness to reflect critically on his or her own behaviour.

2 Charismatic leader Research in leadership and internal branding has emphasized the superiority of a transformational or charismatic in comparison to a transactional leadership. Charismatic leadership as the enhancement of transformational leadership is characterized by the followers' trust in the honesty of the leader, the unquestioning acceptance of the leader, and positive effects for the leader and loyalty (House, 1977). The charismatic leader has an idealized influence, and a high level of inspirational motivation, intellectual stimulation and consideration of individual needs (Bass, 1985). A charismatic leader with a CSR attitude and enthusiasm has a strong impact on the employees' commitment and enthusiasm. Hence, a strong CSR brand is often based on a charismatic leader. Morhart *et al.* (2009) have shown that brand-specific transformational leadership can be learned through management training. However, charisma is a personality trait that cannot be obtained as a formal qualification and thus is hard to imitate in a competitive environment.

The following case study of the Austrian CSR brand Sonnentor exemplifies these leader factors.

CASE STUDY The founder of Sonnentor: Johannes Gutmann

Sonnentor is an Austrian company that specializes in manufacturing and marketing organic herbs, teas and spices. The company was founded in the rural area of Waldviertel in 1988 by Johannes Gutmann. His idea was to sell organically farmed goods to regional and international markets. In 1992, the company set up a subsidiary in the Czech Republic and a cultivation project was started in Romania in 1999.

Sonnentor leads the Austrian market with a 50 per cent market share in the specialized organic trade (tea and spices, not including food trade). In Germany, the company holds a 25 per cent market share and ranks in the top three. The products are sold in more than 45 countries all over the world, with a logo of a smiling sun. Germany, the Czech Republic and Switzerland are the main export markets, but Bali, Japan, Malaysia, Hong Kong, Korea and New Zealand are also export destinations. There are 135 employees working at the headquarters of Sonnentor in Austria, and another 60 work at the Czech subsidiary.

Gutmann's quality management requires that all products come from certified organic farming, are free of colour, preservatives and artificial aroma additives, and are carefully processed into over 600 products. Every product can be traced back to the farm where the raw materials were cultivated. The farmers themselves are a part of the manufacturing and packaging process because most of the work is still done by hand. This is how Sonnentor makes sure that the farm workers and co-workers identify with the company philosophy.

In 2008, Sonnentor received the TRIGOS award for its social and environmental commitment to regional suppliers. In addition, for its communicative activities in Eastern Europe, Sonnentor was recognized with a New Territory Award in 2010, and in the 'Neighbourhood' category they also received the Dr. Erwin Pröll Future Prize.

The head of SONNENTOR can be easily distinguished from other classically dressed businessmen. His trademarks are his round, red glasses and his leather trousers. Actually, he did not want to take over his parents' farm, but after his exams he also did not want to live in a big city like Vienna or Linz. So he decided to stay at home. Soon, he developed a logo and packaging for the organic herbal products and sold them on the local markets. Word of mouth made him known and increasingly interesting to the herb growers in the region. They liked Gutmann's idea and started to place the Sonnentor label on their products. Today, Johannes Gutmann tells his story internally and externally. His excitement and mission are well documented in around 700 YouTube videos.

In addition to the personality of the leader, top management influences the internal anchorage of the CSR brand by concrete decisions and the implementation of leadership instruments.

3 CSR-oriented reward and controlling systems Top management is responsible for the implementation of reward and control systems. These formal systems communicate the relevance of topics and values. In addition to that, the outcomes of these systems function as extrinsic incentives for the employees. Hence, reward and control systems, such as an eco-balance or CSR-related key performance indicators, which are implemented and managed on a top management level, have a strong impact on employees' thinking and behaviour.

4 CSR-oriented rules and norms Similar to the reward and control system, top management also decides on rules and norms. These regulate the behaviour of single departments, such as purchasing, production, marketing or sales, or of the whole workforce. The role of top management is not only to formulate, implement and control such rules, but also to exemplify them.

The case example of the German outdoor brand Vaude illustrates these principles in practice.

CASE STUDY Common Good balance sheet and rules by Vaude

Vaude Sport develops, produces and sells outdoor equipment, including functional clothes, backpacks and bags, sleeping bags, tents, footwear and camping equipment. The products of Vaude stand for expertise in mountaineering, innovation, and responsible handling of humans and nature.

Vaude is a family-owned enterprise that was founded by Albrecht von Dewitz in 1974. The initials of the founder's last name were used to compose the company name. Today, the company is under management by the second generation, with Antje von Dewitz serving as CEO. About 500 employees work for Vaude in Tettnang-Obereisenbach in the south of Germany.

In the last few years, Vaude has won several awards for its social and ecological initiatives, the company's economic performance and the brand itself. In 2015, it received the highest honours at the German Sustainability Awards and was named 'Germany's Sustainable Brand 2015'. One important pillar of the internal branding is the use of CSR-related control systems and rules.

For example, Vaude has joined the Economy for the Common Good (ECG) and is publishing an audited Common Good Balance Sheet, which measures business success not only in financial terms but also by the company's contribution to the common good. This includes human dignity, solidarity, environmental sustainability, social justice and democratic participation, and transparency. Vaude achieved a good score in general and particularly in the fields of 'ecological design of products' and 'reducing environmental impact', where Vaude was considered as exemplary. The positive influence of Vaude on the 'increase in the social and environmental industry standards' in the entire outdoor industry was highlighted. Another positive appraisal was that Vaude has taken its first steps in the ECG aspect 'social design of products', such as its cooperation with the organization for collecting old and used clothes, FairWertung, to give used products a second life.

In addition, Vaude has implemented a comprehensive set of internal rules. For example, one rule forbids the marketing department to use a helicopter for outdoor movie shoots. Another rule on mobilization asks all employees to use public transport for business trips. If the use of a company car is necessary, then this rule advocates a careful, thoughtful and fuel-saving driving style.

Human resource management

A second pillar of the internal anchorage of a CSR brand inside the whole workforce of a company is human resource management. Conceptual papers pinpoint the pivotal relevance of the HR department for internal brand management (eg Davis and Dunn, 2002; Hatch and Schultz, 2008; Ind, 2007). In addition, some empirical findings support the significance of the HR department for the success of the internal anchorage of a brand (Aurand *et al.*, 2005). The HR pillar includes the tasks, tools and programmes that are initiated by the human resource department, persons with responsibility for human resource management, or departments with similar responsibilities. The common characteristic is that the internal anchorage is based on a systematic and intentional process (plan and implementation).

The literature on internal brand management offers different lists of instruments. For example, Burmann and Zeplin (2005) differentiate between employer marketing, employee selection and the introduction of new employees. Ind (2007) distinguishes between recruitment and training as well as appraisals and rewards. Sackmann (2010) offers a detailed catalogue of relevant human resource management instruments, from selection and socialization of new employees to personnel development, selection of managers, norms (eg leadership guidelines) and monitoring. The most detailed list of HR instruments in the context of internal brand management was published by Schmeichel (2005). His empirical study in the German banking sector analyses the impact of 13 different HR instruments on brand equity (consumers, potential employees).

In addition to these comprehensive catalogues, several authors discuss individual HR instruments for internal branding in more detail: mentoring (eg Swap *et al.*, 2001), employee empowerment (eg Cuason, 2004) and brand ambassador programmes (eg Anderson and Ekman, 2009).

It is beyond the scope of this chapter to describe all possible instruments in detail. However, the following list discusses pivotal success factors.

1 Collaboration between brand management and HR department   A prerequisite for an effective use of the HR department for internal branding is an open, intensive and equal cooperation between the branding or marketing department on the one side and the HR department on the other. In many companies, these two departments are separated silos that are more engaged in fighting for their own power than collaborating. Hence, the top management, as well as the departments, must create a good atmosphere between the two departments and destroy silo thinking and behaviour. Mixed brand teams, an early integration of the HR department in brand projects, establishment of brand management at the C level (authorized for the marketing, sales and HR departments), job rotation between marketing and HR departments, and spaces for informal conversations are possible approaches to achieve the necessary collaboration.

2 Long-term perspective The goal of all HR actions is to change the thinking and behaviour of all employees in the direction of the CSR brand values. This is based on socialization and a learning process for the employees. These processes need time and continuity. Hence, the HR instruments should have a long-term focus. Short projects or single events are not successful. Programmes with a long-term perspective with continuous updates based on feedback have more impact on internal brand equity.

3 Offerings instead of obligations CSR-related internal programmes should be voluntary; employees often perceive forced programmes as a duty, and the necessary motivation and deep learning are hindered by this attitude. However, the success of HR measurements is based on the integration of as many employees as possible. Hence, the HR department, as well as all managers and employees, must advertise the different offerings internally. Best practices and field reports by former participants (via intranet, employee newsletter, posters) as well as word-of-mouth communication are suitable instruments for internal communication.

4 High-quality and professional implementation Training and other HR instruments achieve maximum effect only if they are delivered professionally and with high quality. Classical coach-centered and classroom teaching are often not very effective and, as didactic approaches, quite old-fashioned. Problem-based learning, interaction and dialogue, stimulating spaces, own experiences with all senses as well as the meaningful mix of classical and new media are the main characteristics of modern and effective learning approaches. Hence, HR programmes should be based on recent insights in adult learning.

In addition to that, the organization of such programmes (eg rooms, trainer, catering, feedback system) should fulfil professional standards.

The next case study illustrates these principles using the CSR brand Weleda.

CASE STUDY HR management as an integral part of the internal branding of Weleda

Weleda is a leading producer of natural cosmetics and anthroposophical pharmaceuticals. It is a Swiss Stock Corporation that was founded in 1921, with its headquarter in Arlesheim in Switzerland. Over 2,000 employees all over the world work in production, development and marketing. The product portfolio contains more than 1,000 pharmaceutical products, several extemporaneous pharmaceutical preparations and 120 natural cosmetics, which are distributed in more than 50 countries. Weleda acts as a forward-looking company with a social commitment that focuses on social, environmental and economic responsibility. The Weleda brand is one of the strongest cosmetic brands worldwide. Several awards (eg Swiss Ethics Award 2016; National German Sustainability Award – Brand 2016; Cosmopolitan Prix de Beauté 2016 – Green Beauty) and market research results underpin Weleda's brand equity for different stakeholder groups.

One main pillar of Weleda brand management is the strong internal anchorage of the brand values and the anthroposophical philosophy of the company. The following list sketches some pivotal building blocks of the personnel development and training programme:

- **Werkstunden**. Regular (every two months) one-hour sessions on current topics (eg flow of refugees, understanding an annual report, principles of Weleda) since 1927.

- **Curriculum 'Identity and values of WELEDA'**. Three × three-day sessions on the philosophy of anthroposophy and the values of WELEDA. Around 250 participants since 2010; international roll-out is scheduled.

- **Identity workshop**. New format, two-hour workshop on the WELEDA brand values. Goal: development of all employees to become brand ambassadors.

- **Family workshops**. Events for employees' whole families; creative and nature-oriented topics like building a bee hotel.

All these initiatives are coordinated by a newly established (2012) concept, 'culture and identity', which links HR, marketing and other departments. For the employees, all these programmes are voluntary and are part of regular working hours.

Internal communication

The last management field for the anchorage of the CSR brand inside the company is internal communication. Several researchers pinpoint the relevance of internal communication for creating internal brand equity (eg Burmann and Zeplin, 2005; Punjaisri and Wilson, 2007).

The first task of communication is to inform the employees about the CSR philosophy and to increase their knowledge about the brand and its values. The second task of communication is to motivate the employees to behave in a brand-consistent way. Finally, the communication should inspire the workforce about their own CSR brand and should create pride in the brand.

To systematize the broad topic of communication, a lot of attributes are available in the literature:

- internal or external communication (both impact on employees);
- media or face-to-face communication;
- fact-based or symbolic communication; or
- top-down or lateral communication.

It is beyond the scope of this chapter to discuss in detail all the different types of communication and their advantages and disadvantages, but overall, we can identify the following success factors.

1 Fact-based communication is not enough In the past, internal and external CSR communication was often dominated by a factual and unemotional style. This is not quite convincing and thus not suitable to build up enthusiasm inside and outside the company (Polyorat *et al.*, 2007). A more effective approach is to use symbols and story-telling to sensitize employees to the brand's relevance and to present the CSR values of the company. Symbols and stories are strong instruments for a more informal and indirect communication (eg Hatch and Schulz, 2003; Ind, 2007; Swap *et al.*, 2001). Such a style of internal communication reduces or even prevents resistance from employees, increases learning and reinforces emotional buy-in. The CSR brand Auro presents a best-practice example for this type of internal communication.

CASE STUDY Symbolic communication in Auro

Auro is a supplier for construction companies (dye industry), founded in 1983 by Dr Hermann Fischer, specializing in ecological paints, impregnations, coatings and glues as well as accompanying ranges such as cleaning, care and maintenance agents. Auro manufactures products principally based on organic and mineral raw materials, and not just as a side assortment alongside a conventional standard product range. The idea is to develop solutions for the post-fossil era.

To communicate the ecological values and the overall philosophy of a 'soft chemistry', the founder of the company has installed conventional symbols such as organic food in the canteen and wooden office furniture. In addition to these symbols, he has integrated a library in the company headquarters stocked with books about the history and development of 'soft chemistry'.

2 Creative, experience-oriented and conspicuous communication
Related to the first argument, an impactful internal CSR communication should try to use creative and surprising approaches. Such a communication approach increases the attention of employees and the chances of an internal word-of-mouth effect. In addition, a direct experience of the brand values can support the 'teaching' and communication effect.

The case of Lichtblick explains such a communication approach for a CSR brand.

CASE STUDY Brand experience room in Lichtblick

With over one million customers, Lichtblick is the leading independent green electricity company in Germany. The company was founded in 1998 by Michael Saalfeld and Heiko von Tschischwitz (current CEO of the company), and in 2010 was awarded the prestigious National German Sustainability Award in the brand category. The company is not only eco-oriented but also very innovative in all areas. Examples like special electricity tariffs for fans of two soccer clubs with a long tradition and a broad fan base (Borussia Dortmund, St. Pauli), implementation of small power stations for private housing, or collaboration with Tesla regarding the commercialization of small and decentralized energy storage systems illustrate the entrepreneurial and innovation orientation of Lichtblick.

In 2015, the company relaunched a refined brand concept. One building block of this concept was a stronger emphasis on brand relevance and brand values inside the company. As a symbol of this, Lichtblick re-worked the canteen at the headquarters in Hamburg to change it from a functional room into a brand experience space.

The space was conceptually segmented into three areas: (1) a lounge area for employees, offering snacks and beverages as well as sitting accommodation for casual meetings; (2) a creative meeting space equipped with state-of-the-art technology for interaction; (3) a corporate section, offering appealing gadgets to engage interactively with the company's identity, history and strategy. The haptic-focused concept of the brand experience space lets the company's DNA come to life, making it accessible to everyone. The intention was to offer both employees and guests a space to dwell and interact in an unbuttoned yet productive way.

3 Long-term, lateral and engaging communication approach The internal anchorage of the CSR brand inside the company is a change and learning process. Therefore, an important characteristic of a persuasive internal CSR brand communication is a long-term perspective. Internal communication should emphasize the values repeatedly. This continuous internal communication can be supported by a combination of top-down, bottom-up and lateral communication. The implementation of an explicit brand ambassador programme can push lateral communication (eg Anderson and Ekman, 2009; Ind, 2007).

4 Value-congruent and accurate communication A final prerequisite of persuasive and involving internal communication is the sincerity and credibility of the messages. An internal communication with incongruent or deceptive messages is likely to confuse employees and destroy their trust and commitment. Hence, internal communication should focus on the formulated CSR brand values and should always and only use accurate information in all situations.

Conclusion

CSR brand management is a complex and multifaceted approach. The creation and maintenance of a strong CSR brand are based on the interplay of C-level activity brand positioning, corporate culture, actual behaviour, and communication to all relevant stakeholders. Such a holistic approach prevents 'greenwashing' and other superficial CSR approaches.

One major building block of a 'real' CSR brand is the corporate culture or the internal anchorage of the CSR brand inside the company. To influence the corporate culture, management can use different approaches and instruments. The most important instruments are leadership, HRM and internal communication, and in this chapter 12 success factors have been discussed and illustrated with short case examples. These factors can be the basis for the development of a comprehensive and long-term 'Living the CSR brand' programme that is designed to embed the CSR brand values. In addition, the list of success factors can be the basis for the evaluation of internal branding activities via a checklist or a more formal brand audit approach (eg Baumgarth *et al.*, 2016).

To sum up, management should always remember that employees can make or break the CSR brand.

References

Aguilera, RV, Rupp, D E, Williams, C A and Ganapathi, J (2007) Putting the s back in corporate social responsibility: A multilevel theory of social change in organizations, *Academy of Management Review*, **32** (3), pp. 836–63

Anderson, M and Ekman, P (2009) Ambassador networks and place branding, *Journal of Place Management and Development*, **2** (1), pp. 41–51

Angus-Leppan, T, Metcalf, L and Benn, S (2010) Leadership styles and CSR practice: An examination of sensemaking, institutional drivers and CSR leadership, *Journal of Business Ethics*, **93** (2), pp. 189–213

Aurand, T W, Gorchels, L and Bishop, T T (2005) Human resource management's role in internal branding: An opportunity for cross-functional brand message synergy, *Journal of Product & Brand Management*, **14** (3), pp. 163–69

Bass, B M (1985) *Leadership and Performance Beyond Expectations*, New York: Free Press

Baumgarth, C (2010) 'Living the brand': Brand orientation in the business-to-business sector, *European Journal of Marketing*, **44** (5), pp. 653–71

Baumgarth, C and Binckebanck, L (2011) Sales force impact on b-to-b brand equity: Conceptual framework and empirical test, *Journal of Product and Brand Management*, **20** (6), pp. 487–98

Baumgarth, C and Binckebanck, L (2015) *Building and managing CSR brands: Theory and applications*, Proceedings of the International Conference on Corporate Social Responsibility & Sustainable Business Development, Ho-Chi-Minh-City: VNU-HCM Press, pp. 35–51

Baumgarth, C, Kaluza, M and Lohrisch, N (2016) Brand audit for cultural institutions (BAC): A validated and holistic brand controlling tool, *International Journal of Arts Management*, **19** (1), pp. 54–68

Becker-Olsen, K L, Taylor, C R, Hill, R P and Yalcinkaya, G (2011) A cross-cultural examination of corporate social responsibility marketing communications in Mexico and the United States: Strategies for global brands, *Journal of International Marketing*, **19** (2), pp.30–44

Bernal, E (2016) Exploiting leadership to better the world, in Ind N and Horlings, S (eds.) *Brands with a Conscience: How to build a successful and responsible brand,* London, Philadelphia: Kogan Page, pp. 199–202

Burmann, C and Zeplin, S (2005) Building brand commitment: A behavioural approach to internal brand management, *Journal of Brand Management*, **12** (4), pp. 279–300

Burmann, C, Zeplin, S and Riley, N (2009) Key determinants of internal brand management success: An exploratory empirical analysis, *Journal of Brand Management*, **16** (4), pp. 264–84

Clarkson, M B E (1995) A stakeholder framework for analyzing and evaluating corporate social performance, *Academy of Management Review*, **20** (1), pp. 92–117

Cuason, J (2004) The internal brand: Successful cultural change and employee empowerment, *Journal of Change Management*, 4 (4), pp. 297–307

Davis, S M and Dunn, M (2002) *Building the Brand-driven Business*, San Francisco: Jossey-Bass

de Chernatony, L (2010) From Brand Vision to Brand Evaluation (3rd edn), oxford: Butterworth-Heinemann

Einwiller, S and Will, M (2002) Towards an integrated approach to corporate branding: An empirical study, *Corporate Communications*, 7 (2), pp. 100–109

Ellen, P S, Webb, D J and Mohr, L A (2006) Building corporate associations: Consumer attributions for corporate socially responsible programs, *Journal of the Academy of Marketing Science*, 34 (2), pp. 147–57

Gelb, B D and Rangarajan, D (2014) Employee contributions to brand equity, *California Management Review*, 56 (2), pp. 95–112

Godfrey, P C, Merrill, C B and Hansen, J M (2009) The relationship between corporate social responsibility and shareholder value: An empirical test of the risk management hypothesis, *Strategic Management Review*, 30 (4), pp. 425–45

Gromark, J and Melin, F (2011) The underlying dimensions of brand orientation and its impact on financial performance, *Journal of Brand Management*, 18 (6), pp. 394–410

Hatch, M J and Schultz, M (2001) Are the strategic stars aligned for your corporate brand? *Harvard Business Review*, 79 (2), pp. 128–34

Hatch, M J and Schultz, M (2003) Bringing the corporation into corporate branding, *European Journal of Marketing*, 37 (7/8), pp. 1041–64

Hatch, M J and Schultz, M (2008) Taking Brand Initiative, San Francisco: Jossey-Bass

Hillestad, T, Xie, C and Haugland, S A (2010) Innovative corporate social responsibility: The founder's role in creating a trustworthy corporate brand through 'green innovation', *Journal of Product & Brand Management*, 19 (6), pp. 440–51

Homburg, C and Pflesser, C (2000) A multiple-layer model of market-oriented organizational culture: Measurement issues and performance outcomes, *Journal of Marketing Research*, 37 (4), pp. 449–62

Homburg, C, Stierl, M and Bornemann, T (2013) Corporate social responsibility in business-to-business markets: How organizational customers account for supplier corporate social responsibility engagement, *Journal of Marketing*, 77 (6), pp. 54–72

House, R J (1977) A 1976 theory of charismatic leadership, in Hunt, J G and Larson, L (eds.) *Leadership: The cutting edge*, Carbondale: Southern Illinois University Press, pp. 189–207

Ind, N (2007) *Living the Brand: How to transform every member of your organization into a brand champion* (3rd edn). London: Kogan Page

Keller, K L and Richey, K (2006) The importance of corporate brand personality traits to a successful 21st century business, *Journal of Brand Management*, 14 (1–2), pp. 74–81

Matanda, M J and Ndubisi, N O (2013) Internal marketing, internal branding, and organisational outcomes: The moderating role of perceived goal congruence, *Journal of Marketing Management*, 29 (9–10), pp. 1030–55

Miles, S J and Mangold, G (2004) A conceptualization of the employee branding process, *Journal of Relationship Marketing*, 3 (2/3), pp. 65–87

Morhart, F M, Herzog, W and Tomczak, T (2009) Brand-specific leadership: Turning employees into brand champions, *Journal of Marketing*, 73 (5), pp. 122–42

Palazzo, G and Basu, K (2007) The ethical backlash of corporate branding, *Journal of Business Ethics*, 73 (4), pp. 333–46

Polyorat, K, Alden, D and Kim, E S (2007) Impact of narrative versus factual print ad copy on product evaluation: The mediating role of ad message involvement, *Psychology & Marketing*, 24 (6), pp. 539–54

Punjaisri, K and Wilson, A (2007) The role of internal branding in the delivery of employee brand promise, *Journal of Brand Management*, 15 (1), pp. 57–70

Punjaisri, K and Wilson, A (2011) Internal branding process: Key mechanisms, outcomes and moderating factors, *European Journal of Marketing*, 45 (9–10), pp. 1521–37

Sackmann, S A (2010) Markenorientierte Führung und Personalmanagement [Brand oriented leadership and HR management] in Krobath, K and Schmidt, H J (eds.), *Innen Beginen* [Start Internally], Wiesbaden: Gabler, pp. 47–59

Schein, E H (1999) *Corporate Culture Survival Guide*, San Francisco: Jossey-Bass

Schein, E H (2004) *Organizational Culture and Leadership* (3rd edn) San Francisco: Jossey-Bass

Schmeichel, C (2005) *Personalmanagement als Instrument zur Markenbildung im Privatkundengeschäft von Kreditinstituten: Eine kausalanalytische Betrachtung* [HR management as an instrument for internal branding in the private banking sector: A causal analytic approach], München & Mering: Rainer Hamp

Sen, S and Bhattacharya, C B (2001) Does doing good always lead to doing better? Consumer reactions to corporate social responsibility, *Journal of Marketing Research*, **38** (2), pp. 225–43

Swap, W, Leonard, D, Shields, M and Abrams, L (2001) Using mentoring and storytelling to transfer knowledge in the workplace, *Journal of Management Information Systems*, **18** (1), pp. 95–114

Urde, M (1999) Brand orientation: A mindset for building brands into strategic resources, *Journal of Marketing Management*, **15** (1–3), pp. 117–33

Urde, M, Baumgarth, C and Merrilees, B (2013) Brand orientation and market orientation: From alternatives to synergy, *Journal of Business Research*, **66** (1), pp. 13–20

Vallaster, C and de Chernatony, L (2006) Internal brand building and structuration: The role of leadership, *European Journal of Marketing*, **40** (7/8), pp. 761–84

Vallaster, C, Lindgreen, A and Maon, F (2012) Strategically leveraging corporate social responsibility: A corporate branding perspective, *California Management Review*, **54** (3), pp. 34–60

Wallace, E and de Chernatony, L (2008) Classifying, identifying and managing the service brand saboteur, *The Service Industries Journal*, **28** (2), pp. 151–65

Participation builds the brand: VSO's people brand

08

NICK PULLAN AND HANNAH GILMAN

Introduction

In 1958 Alec and Moira Dickson recruited and sent 16 British volunteers overseas to teach English in Borneo. This was the beginning of Voluntary Service Overseas (VSO). Since then, thousands of volunteers have worked on international development programmes in more than 120 countries. Now VSO recruits volunteers with specialist skills such as hospital management and curriculum advice – skills that are much harder to recruit, particularly to unpaid volunteer positions, not least because the ideal candidates have careers, families, mortgages and other commitments. VSO also has to compete with paid employment, overseas paid consultant roles and other charities.

To meet the needs of the countries it works with, VSO has developed a federated structure with bases in the Netherlands, Ireland, Philippines, Kenya and the UK, where the head office is based. Traditionally each of these bases recruited and trained its own volunteers and employees. Volunteers could then be sent to placements in any of the countries where VSO had programmes, working alongside volunteers from other VSO recruitment bases. The advantages of this were many, but particularly evident in South–South volunteering where volunteers often had experienced similar conditions in their home country to those in which they were now living and working. More recently VSO has implemented a new model of international recruitment, which has improved effectiveness by enabling it to recruit globally across borders, opening up many new opportunities for sourcing both employees and volunteers in countries where previously it had not been able to recruit. However, the clear problem in implementing the new model has been lack of awareness of the organization or what it could offer individuals in new markets.

While VSO has a robust corporate brand, there has been a lack of visibility, especially among potential employees and volunteers. To improve its appeal, VSO set out to define a global employer brand. From the outset, it was clear that the employer brand needed to stem from the corporate values and vision but with tailored communications for employees and volunteers. Therefore, as far as possible VSO had to integrate the language and intentions of the two elements. This was important to achieve synergy and acceptance among managers.

People are the face of VSO, so one of the goals of this project was to engage everyone to become brand champions and advocates. VSO wanted to ensure that the right people were joining the organization and that once they were part of the team, it was easy for them to become spokespeople. Everyone at VSO has the potential to be a champion but also a critic, so developing a strong employer brand was important to allow the organization to recognize the enormous efforts and impact of employees and volunteers. By allowing people to praise and critique the charity, changes could be made to improve the experience of joining and then working and developing within VSO.

The purpose of VSO's People Brand

As with many other charities, VSO employees who work in central functions (head offices) sometimes feel disconnected from the volunteers and the on-the-ground work that they support. Inevitably perhaps there are misunderstandings and assumptions. Volunteers can feel that decisions affecting their work are made without their input and those who are office based are often unsure how best to engage hundreds of people scattered around the globe. To bring a greater sense of cohesion, VSO decided it was important to bring everybody under one umbrella. To reflect this, at an early stage, VSO decided to discard the description of Employer Brand and to call it a People Brand. Instead of treating employees and volunteers as two different groups (often the distinction is unclear), the goal was to bring them together as 'VSO People' to create one unified and powerful workforce. VSO also believed that by improving internal communications it would be possible to bring the impact of work closer through stories, messages and impact statistics that reflected the passion and commitment of everyone involved.

The timing of the People Brand project came at a turning point in attitudes towards remote working at VSO. The IT department was making huge strides in enabling colleagues in different countries to collaborate. VSO had started using a whole range of tools to allow online discussions, conference video and calls and internal messaging. These meetings were by no means seamless, with plenty of growling at devices that didn't respond, but with perseverance and patience issues became few and far between.

Technology was key in enabling the People Brand to develop with widespread engagement from all around the world. Holding online meetings with contributors for example from Ethiopia, Ireland, Myanmar and Kenya all sharing ideas did more for the success of the project than any number of e-mails and intranet articles could have done. If the organization was all about people as it claimed, it needed to connect people so that each individual could feel part of a whole.

To get to this point, one thing was clear: you could not simply tell people, they needed to be part of the process and understand what the project was going to give them. It was also clear that whatever the brand looked and felt like, it needed to be reflected in changing practices. Pretty rhetoric would soon be found out and in an organization focused on improving the lives of the very poorest people in the world, a project that could be seen as just empty words and pictures would soon be shot down. Hand in hand with the brand development, VSO was focusing on application processes, reviewing digital presence and improving management and training tools.

People Brand is more than HR

VSO's overall strategy *People First* seeks to put the right people in the right place at the right time, in order to transform lives and communities. But there was low awareness of VSO outside the international development sphere, so attracting the right people in a crowded marketplace was difficult.

Far from being seen as an HR 'issue' and therefore driven solely by this team, VSO recognized that becoming an employer of choice required deep-seated change within the organization and across its various functions. A key factor in the success of the project was the high-level support that the project was given by the communications, volunteering and HR heads of department. By recognizing the importance of building a strong People Brand, these leaders championed through their actions the involvement of colleagues throughout the organization.

The People Brand project wasn't hidden away from view, but kept vibrant in team briefings, newsletters, intranet articles and through coffee machine discussions. The latter were often the most useful in ironing out hostile or negative attitudes to the project.

An immediate benefit of working across teams was seeing new working relationships forming. Colleagues shared their work practices and challenges and ideas were shared and discussed. 'I am really excited to be able to contribute to this project as it's not something I usually get involved in' was an often-expressed feeling from participants.

By encouraging people within VSO to come on board and contribute, it became much easier to identify and develop those brand assets that would allow VSO to better recruit and retain volunteers and employees. Retention doesn't stop when people transition into alumni – as ambassadors for VSO, many employees and volunteers remain keen supporters of the organization, whether through advocacy, fundraising or rejoining in new posts, so keeping them connected to VSO was critical too.

Process of developing the People Brand

How do you start developing a People Brand that is relevant and inspirational to people from over 100 countries, speaking different languages and working in very different environments? When there is already so much change going on, how can you ask for time and effort on something new? VSO needed a coherent brand that would be easily recognized and would stand out. However, it needed to be flexible enough to allow for regional differences and requirements.

The last thing VSO needed was another head office-driven project. Early on in the process, the decision was taken to start from the outside in, working with the local country offices and building on the outcomes from there before working with regional hubs. The strategy was very successful for two reasons: the country offices appreciated that they were not faced with a 'fait accompli' but were really driving the project from the start; and regional hubs were presented with clear recommendations and facts from the very people they were supporting, which helped to steer workshops and discussions.

Kick-off workshops were held in Papua New Guinea, Myanmar and Nigeria, where both volunteers and employees took part in a series of workshops to define VSO's brand. During these workshops the employees and volunteers came together to take part in training on the importance of brand, analysing local competition, reviewing media outputs and identifying communication strategies. Participants provided impact stories and images to illustrate the people brand.

The make-up of the workshop participants was crucial here: everyone was invited, from country managers to reception staff, volunteers and programme leaders. Planning and executing these local workshops was a feat of organization as many volunteers were based a long way from the country offices, with little online or phone communication. Planning how to get them to a workshop, without incurring travel costs, was difficult. In addition, facilities were often basic, but this added to the creativity of the sessions. Most of the stimulus materials used were prepared and brought from the UK, meaning a luggage allowance mainly taken up of magazines, glue, Post-it notes and sweets (the latter essential for creative thinking!).

These regional workshops provided the raw materials to start building the People Brand, but other consultations were held with specific purposes. VSO held a week-long online forum for key influencers in the organization – individuals who had been identified as those they'd like to have more of at VSO! Daily topics and questions were posted, delving into reasons for joining (and staying with) VSO. Individual consultations were also held with directors and senior managers, looking at the issues they faced within their teams. A workshop for recent recruits focused specifically on employer branding in the sector. All in all, over 500 people contributed their thoughts to the process and many, many more were aware of and able to follow developments through newsletters, team briefings and articles.

Pulling it all together

It soon became apparent from the different discussions that there was one recurring big idea that reflected VSO's people and that was 'inspiring'. This led to the core People Brand theme of *Inspiring People*. This has a dual meaning in that VSO's employees and volunteers are themselves inspiring and what they do is inspire others to make change happen. It reflects the participative way that VSO works with people, communities and governments. VSO inspires others to deliver change.

When the idea of *Inspiring People* was first revealed, some reactions showed that many volunteers really did not want to be seen as inspiring; they didn't feel they deserved that accolade. This is a reflection of the altruistic nature of much of their work, which is done to support others, rather than for personal gains. Yet as the *Inspiring People* idea was discussed and developed, volunteers and employees saw it as a powerful way to attract and retain people. They also appreciated the flexibility that came through as the central idea was expanded. Through the workshops and consultations, several themes emerged that captured the various elements that reflected the 'VSO experience'. These eight sub-themes ('building blocks'), added the flexibility that allowed different elements of VSO's work to be highlighted depending on the situation.

Implementation

Having agreed *Inspiring People* and the idea of the building blocks, VSO moved into the implementation phase. The goal here was to develop a series of recruitment and management messages and behaviours that ensured that from the first interaction with VSO the organization

Figure 8.1 VSO's core People Brand theme and the eight building blocks

came across as engaging and motivating. To start this process, VSO undertook a touch point analysis that assessed the current and ideal points of interaction between the organization and volunteers from searching for a job or placement, to team meetings and training.

After working through the full lifecycle of touch points and key channels used to communicate with prospective, current and former employees and volunteers, VSO developed a set of user guidelines to show how to communicate key messages and reinforce the brand at each point of contact. The guidelines included details on the look and feel of the brand, along with a toolkit containing copy and templates for recruitment and in-post materials such as banners, flyers and brochures. It also outlined the implications for employee and volunteer behaviours.

To improve adoption and effectiveness, flexibility was built in to the guidelines so that the brand could be adapted to suit local circumstances while still maintaining a globally consistent picture of VSO.

The flexibility of the building blocks enabled recruiters to build campaigns around one or more specific area of focus, tied in to *Inspiring People*, to suit the context. For example, when creating a job advert a recruiter might base it around the elements of *Enabling Innovation* and *Sharing Knowledge* or of *Demonstrating Passion, Showing Impact* and *Building Relationships*. The interchangeable nature of the blocks provided excellent scope for adapting to specific requirements, coming in handy for the diversity of geographies and roles being recruited, such as paediatric surgeons, education advisors, microfinance specialists, criminal lawyers, and organizational development managers.

In May 2015, the guidelines were launched and made accessible online to everyone in the organization. Dedicated training was provided, principally through remote means, for specific groups such as recruiters and people managers in all the country offices. The training covered both the People and Corporate Brands, their relationship and when to use each. This combined approach was valuable, in that many of the individuals involved had never received any specific training on the Corporate Brand and so this brought benefits beyond just the employer angle.

It was also an opportunity to remind everyone about the services and support available from the communications team, which was particularly helpful for country offices with limited in-house marketing and communications expertise.

Previously, there had been no central storage facility for recruitment marketing materials and so it had been difficult for recruiters to know what collateral had been produced by other offices. To rectify this, an online global repository was created to allow easier sharing. Not only did this save time as recruiters could adapt and re-use content which had already been created elsewhere within VSO but it also reinforced consistency.

Furthermore, it was one of the tools through which brand usage was closely monitored in the first few months after launch, with additional support offered where needed to ensure that people complied with the new guidelines.

Figure 8.2   Example of VSO People Brand Recruitment Poster

Challenges

Implementation was not without its difficulties. Three factors in particular held back both the roll out and uptake: geography, corporate direction and restructure.

1 Geographical footprint

VSO has 25 offices across Africa, Asia and Europe and sources candidates from over 100 countries. The organization needed a value proposition that would bring together VSO's diversity and represent it as a whole but would also be sufficiently adaptable so that national and regional offices felt that they truly owned the brand and could make effective use of it.

Not only was there a need to factor in variances in the culture and means of attracting and engaging talent across so many locations but there were practical considerations for the research and implementation phases.

Many volunteers were based in remote communities without basic services, let alone internet connections. Allowing them all to feel fully involved in the process was unrealistic but participation was encouraged through careful planning, giving those places longer deadlines to return surveys, and by taking advantage of situations to talk as opportunities arose.

Finding effective ways for the small project team to deliver the relatively in-depth brand training to all VSO recruiters and HR business partners, located across multiple time zones and with unreliable connectivity, proved to be a relentless process. Providing online access to the Guidelines, FAQs and templates helped, as did the repository to allow sharing of brand collateral between offices, but persistence in training and follow-up had the biggest impact in overcoming this challenge.

2 Corporate position and direction

After the People Brand research phase, a review of VSO's global positioning within the international development sector was also initiated.

Although run separately, a benefit of conducting the two projects was that each project was able to share with and learn from the other. For example, feedback gathered through the People Brand workshops, surveys and forum proved a valuable asset for the corporate project team. It helped create an understanding of the sentiment and beliefs of those within the organization – determining how they viewed VSO, what had attracted them to it in the first place and what value they considered the organization brought to the world.

However, as the aim was to design a People Brand which stemmed from the Corporate Brand, and much was unknown or uncertain about the latter's future while it was in a state of flux, this was not straightforward. To help ensure coherence the People Brand was aligned with the organization's mission and values so that whatever direction the new corporate positioning took, the People Brand would remain valid and relevant.

As it wasn't clear how much, if any, of the work might need to be redesigned based on the outcome of the corporate positioning project, this also had the effect of reducing the momentum and senior-level backing given to the People Brand launch.

3 Major change and restructure

While the team was able to plan in advance for the issue of dispersed geography, and to create a People Brand aligned with the organization's mission and values, a restructure of the organization caused the largest block.

A review of the form and focus of the organization, along with a requirement to make significant cost savings, led, amongst other changes, to a large number of redundancies. Phased across all functions, the consultation process for these redundancies began while the People Brand was still being designed.

As a result, the mood was understandably low, especially in the teams and offices being hit hardest by the loss of staff.

Engagement has historically been very high at VSO but coming at a time of lower-than-normal morale made the People Brand a very sensitive topic. Despite a great deal of positive feedback about the new brand, its messaging and strong associations at the organizational level, circumstances made it hard for many employees to buy in to it on a personal level. This had the potential to derail the brand work relating to engagement, retention and internally promoting the values of the organization. It required careful management, and due to these sensitivities and to avoid aggravating the issue, the brand was given a softer launch than would have otherwise been the case.

While the restructure held back, at least in the short term, the impact of the brand internally and made it harder for the behaviours side of the branding to be embedded, externally it did little to limit success. As well as leading to improvements in VSO's recruitment statistics and position as an employer of choice, the People Brand went on to be shortlisted for numerous awards.

Results

Despite the challenges, there were many positive outcomes that came with the development of the new People Brand. It provided a strong platform on which VSO could compete more effectively and more consistently in the global labour market, offering a marked improvement in ability to source, engage and retain talent.

In the year that followed launch, benefits included:

- a growth in awareness of VSO as an employer of choice in existing and new markets;
- an increase in attraction of quality candidates;
- an extended reach of the corporate brand;
- a more cohesive proposition with which to build relationships with sourcing partners;
- a central theme which connected and motivated individuals both internally and externally to the organization's cause.

In particular, it has been effective in the following areas.

Engagement

- **Individuals.** There was a clear emotional buy-in to the proposition and it provided a connected approach for engaging with individuals throughout their involvement with VSO.
- **Partners.** It helped position VSO better amongst its existing and potential sourcing partners.

Consistency

With the brand guidelines and training made accessible across the network of countries, it enabled a more globally consistent picture of VSO to be presented while still allowing locally relevant adaptation.

Alignment with corporate brand

Even if the Corporate Brand changes tack, the People Brand's relevance and validity should remain.

Attraction of applicants

There was a marked increase in:

- click-through from job boards to VSO's application forms;
- direct visits to the VSO website and the volunteering/careers pages;
- the volume of actual applications.

To assess if the new brand had gained traction and awareness since its launch, comparison of the first three months after brand launch to the subsequent three months using web analytics showed the following:

- **Click-through rate from our adverts on external job boards** – increased by 42 per cent.

- **Traffic to employee and volunteer recruitment pages on VSO website** – increased by 38 per cent.

Comparisons made for the first six months post launch (ie May–Oct 15) to the same six months of the previous year using applicant tracking software provided a further demonstration of its impact:

- **Average number of applications received per job advertised** – increased by 41 per cent.

- **Total applications received** – increased by 24 per cent (from 16,525 to 20,512, despite 11 per cent fewer jobs advertised).

- Number of countries from which applications were received – increased from 111 to 135 countries.

Presence/new market penetration

The new brand has been a contributory factor in:

- increasing awareness in existing labour markets;
- building global presence, leading to significant growth in sourcing from new markets.

Recognition

VSO's talent is drawn from many different industries, not just the not-for-profit sector. The brand's look and feel was therefore intentionally developed in a way which would allow the organization to stand out to a multi-sector and international audience.

Achieving this aim brought external recognition, with VSO being shortlisted for several top employer branding and recruitment awards, beating a host of globally recognized private and public organizations.

Crucially, the People Brand itself also recognized the contribution made by VSO People.

In contrast to the successes, the lack of emphasis put into embedding behavioural change during roll-out due to the large restructure reduced the anticipated impact in that respect. This behaviours piece had been a key driver for the new brand and so represented a failure in the short term. However, it still offered the basis for incorporating that emphasis in the longer term.

Overall, development of the People Brand created an engaging proposition and provided a powerful representation of VSO and it did this by harnessing the passion and loyalty its people have for the organization.

Forged around a simple, inspirational and aspirational idea, it showcased the attributes and qualities that make VSO distinctive.

Living brands: 09
the characteristics
of living brand
companies

RIK RIEZEBOS

In organizational branding, it is commonly believed that the image and the reputation of a corporate brand are largely determined by external communications such as PR and corporate communications. In practice, however, the perceptions of a company may to a strong degree be determined by its (internal) characteristics. Consequently, when building a corporate brand, one should start with a thorough diagnosis of the organization behind the brand. In this chapter, we elaborate upon a model that may help managers to get to know their company better, so as to make decisions on what branding techniques may work – and not work.

Introduction

In 1995, Jeffrey Pfeffer published the article 'Producing sustainable competitive advantage through the effective management of people'. In it, he posed the question: what discriminates extraordinarily successful companies – in terms of profit and market domination – from others? To answer the question, Pfeffer referred to Porter (1985) who had established five conditions for competitive advantage. In his article, however, unlike Porter, Pfeffer reasoned backwards. He looked at companies that had been highly successful, and tried to determine what these high-performing companies had in common. He came to the conclusion that, in the period from 1972 to 1992, the most successful American companies did not comply to the conditions that were described by Porter. Pfeffer established that for the five best-performing companies in that period (Southwest Airlines, Wal-Mart, Tyson Foods, Circuit City and Plenum Publishing) the pivotal difference was found in the way *they manage their workforce*.[1] Building on Pfeffer's work, Cameron and Quinn (1999) then argued that what lies at the heart of successful companies is a strong *organizational culture*. In 1982, long before Pfeffer and Cameron and Quinn came to their conclusions, Peters and Waterman noted in their search for excellent companies that 'treating people – not money, machines, or minds – as the natural resource may be the key to it all'. Despite these 'early' findings on the positive effect of a motivated workforce on the external perceptions of a company, it is still not a widespread belief that organizational culture has a significant influence on the external perception of a brand.

Cameron and Quinn drew upon the article by Pfeffer to make clear that, in order to grow, companies need to focus on changing their organizational culture. In their book *Diagnosing and Changing Organizational Culture* they illustrate the power of a culture change by the so-called Nummi case (New United Motor Manufacturing Inc), based on a factory located in Fremont, California. Until 1985, General Motors (GM) produced the Chevrolet Nova in this factory.[2] In that year, GM and Toyota together established Nummi as a collaborative production facility for GM's Geo Prizm and Toyota's Corolla. Before Toyota stepped in, the average level of absenteeism of the GM-owned plant amounted to as much as 20 per cent each year. After 1985, through the participation of Toyota, this figure dropped to 2 per cent (Cameron and Quinn, 2012 p.14). Even the three to four wildcat strikes per year that GM was confronted with before 1985 completely disappeared when Toyota took over control. Also, the productivity doubled and the quality of the cars became the highest in the GM corporation.

The power of the organizational culture of Toyota was later described by Liker (2004), Liker and Meier (2006), and Liker and Hoseus (2008). Liker (2004) summarized 'the Toyota way' with four Ps, one of which stands for 'People and Partners; respect, challenge, and grow them'.[3] With this case, Cameron and Quinn (1999) try to make clear that companies can only outperform their competitors if: (a) their internal culture is characterized by a collective identity and commitment (shared values and norms); (b) employees (or better, organizational 'members') know what is to be expected from them; and (c) employees all adhere to one and the same sparkling, motivating vision.

Interestingly, most marketers would argue that the starting point for success in any kind of business lies outside the company (ie by profiling it in a unique way in the market). Yet Cameron and Quinn made it clear that the key driver for growth is organizational culture. Or in marketing terms, how well the *delivery* (of the goods or services) lives up to the *promise* made by (marketing) communications. One could, for example conclude that at Toyota, employees are really living up to the values of the brand. In such companies, brand values are not solely used for external communications, they are also used to motivate and empower employees. We refer to companies that employ their brand values successfully – both internally and externally – as *living brands*.[4] Employees working at these companies often behave as 'brand advocates' or, as Morhart *et al.* (2009) call them, *brand champions* – individuals who, even in their private life, generate positive word of mouth for the brand they work for.

Living brands can be found in all kind of places and industries, including business-to-consumer and business-to-business, big and small companies and old and relatively young organizations. Although organizations may change in time, one could cite names such as Apple (described by Van Dyck, 2016), Google (Bock, 2015), Patagonia (Ind, 2007), Pixar (Catmull, 2008), Starbucks (Schultz and Yong, 1997; Schultz and Gordon, 2012), Southwest Airlines (Pfeffer, 1995; Freiberg and Freiberg 1997), Toyota (Liker, 2004; Liker and Meier, 2006; Liker and Hoseus, 2008), and Zappos (Hsieh, 2013), as living brands.

In this chapter, we will explore the characteristics of living brand companies. We will do so by describing a model – the so-called *Brand/Reputation Grid* – in which various research findings on four types of organizations are summarized, and of which one type can be labelled as the 'living brand organization'. Besides living brand organizations, we will describe three other types of organization. In this way, we can make clear in what way living brand organizations deviate from other types of organization (and explore their unique characteristics), and we can formulate guidelines for other types of organization on how to transform themselves into living brands. In doing so, we will first elaborate upon a model that served as stepping stone in developing the Brand/Reputation Grid.

The Brand/Image Grid

The Brand/Reputation Grid is a model that was originally based on the so-called Brand/Image Grid, in which a distinction is made between the internal and the external brand image of a company (Riezebos, 2001). In this model, the *external* image refers to the image that a company has with its (potential) clients. In case of *internal* brand image, we refer to the image that an organization – mostly as an employer – has with its own employees: what do they think about the company they work for? For both dimensions, we distinguish two values: weak vs. strong. On the basis of these two dimensions, a matrix or grid emerges as shown in Figure 9.1. As the independent variable is usually placed on the x-axis in grids (and the dependent variable on the y-axis), we have plotted 'internal brand image' to the x-axis, based on the belief that the external brand image is to a large degree dependent on the organizational culture, or, in other words, the internal brand image. In the grid, we distinguish four types of corporate brands: Personality Brands, Show Brands, Nerd Brands and Blank Brands.

Figure 9.1   The Brand/Image Grid

SOURCE Reizebos (2001)

In the case of a *Blank Brand*, both the internal and the external brand image of an organization have not been sufficiently developed. For both customers and employees, this type of organization does not add value to the product or service that is being delivered. Here the brand is almost non-existent or is marginalized to 'just a logo'. The brand is not used to persuade customers and/or to motivate employees. The label 'Blank Brand' emphasizes that the brand has hardly been developed and thus has little or no meaning to either customers or employees.

A *Show Brand* is characterized by a weak internal and a strong external brand image. Often this emerges in cases where companies paint too rosy a picture of themselves externally. As a consequence, the external promise may not be recognized by employees. Subsequently they may find it difficult to deliver on the promise and may even feel alienated from the company. Feelings of lethargy and resignation may then become stronger than feelings of pride and empowerment. The label 'Show Brand' expresses that the brand looks better on the outside than on the inside.

For *Nerd Brands*, the external image lags behind the internal image. Often this kind of company undersells itself by using an 'understatement' of what they do. Although such companies may deliver a great product or service, they find it hard to tell and convince (potential) clients of their unique offerings. Therefore, customers will not always recognize it as the best offering in the market, although to some it has the appeal of a 'best-kept secret'. In most cases, employees will be proud of the product/service they deliver but their attitude is often quite down to earth. The label 'Nerd Brand' clearly expresses that the focus lies on the quality of the product or service, and not on telling people about its superior value.

Personality Brands can be found at organizations that are characterized by a strong internal and a strong external brand image. From a branding and reputation perspective, this reflects the ideal position for most companies. The majority of customers will most likely label this type of company as the best offering in the market and recommend it to family and friends. In the customer–employee relationship, employees may be seen as both the cause and the consequence. Motivated and enthusiastic employees will deliver a WOW! service (as illustrated by, for example, Zappos) (Hsieh, 2013) and through that add superior value to the product or service for customers. On the other hand, extremely satisfied customers will give employees the feeling that they matter, which may increase employees' pride in the company. Employees will consequently most likely identify themselves with the vision, mission and identity of the company. The label 'Personality Brands' indicates that we are dealing here with a very well-developed and well-executed brand philosophy, which employees and customers may label as a unique 'personality'.

One should take three critical notes into account when using and applying a matrix like the Brand/Image Grid. First, both underlying dimensions are shown as a dichotomy (weak versus strong). In reality these dimensions form a continuous scale. For reasons of structure and to theorize upon differences between companies, we have chosen to use the dichotomies. Second, a big company with several departments may hold different positions in the grid, depending among others things on how employees in different departments experience differences in internal culture. And third, the position of a company in the grid may change over time. Despite the 'shortcomings' of a matrix, the Brand/Image Grid may be of help in tuning the internal and external image to each other. In each position in the grid, the internal and external image of a brand should not widely differ. Overpromising to the outside market may in any quadrant lead to feelings of disorientation among employees. Likewise, under-promising may inhibit feelings of pride among employees. One of the takeaways of this matrix is to keep an eye on the gap between the internal and the external image of one's brand; preferably these images should not grow apart.

After drawing up the Brand/Image Grid, we came to realize that brand images are not always solely determined by a company's efforts in terms of internal and external communications. For example, for a Show Brand, it seems that management often attaches more value to the external brand image of the company than to the internal culture. And in the case of Nerd Brands it could be that the focus is (too much) on product quality, and people forget to tell the outside world how great their product or service is. We assume that these differences in attention are a reflection of the prevailing business orientation, often established by the founder of the company or its current board of directors. To better understand the underlying dimensions of the Brand/Image Grid, we therefore elaborated upon different taxonomies of business orientation. In the next section, we will elaborate upon two dichotomies of business orientation; one within the domain of marketing management and one within strategic management. We will relate these dichotomies to the Brand/Image Grid and use this grid and the two dichotomies on business orientation as a basis for a more comprehensive model that we have called the *Brand/Reputation Grid*.[5]

Two dichotomies of business orientation

In marketing science, a dichotomy is used to illustrate the essentials of marketing. This dichotomy concerns market-oriented vs. product-oriented companies (Kohli and Jaworski, 1990; Narver and Slater, 1990). Narver and Slater define market orientation as 'the organization culture that most effectively and efficiently creates the necessary behaviours for the creation of superior value for buyers and, thus, continuous superior performance for the business'. According to their view, market-oriented companies are strongly focused on customers, competitors and on the inter-functional coordination of market information. Product-oriented companies on the other hand are more focused on product quality and on attaining resources to continuously improve that quality. Gebhardt *et al.* (2006) report on a model that identifies four path-dependent stages for changing a product-oriented company into a more market-oriented one.

The dichotomy of market-oriented vs. product-oriented companies closely resembles a paradox used in strategic management literature, called 'the paradox of markets and resources' (referring to market and product orientation respectively) (De Wit and Meyer, 2014). The market-based view is also referred to as an *outside-in* way of setting up and running a business, where the resource-based view is seen as an *inside-out* way of doing business. Companies that act on a market-based view will often describe their competitive advantage as 'being best able to respond to the needs and desires in the market'. Usually these companies will adapt themselves to, and respond swiftly to changes in the market. Companies that are acting

Figure 9.2   Terms used in marketing and strategic management for two types of business orientation

	Inside-out	Outside-in
Marketing management	Product orientation	Market orientation
Strategic management	Resource-based view	Market-based view

on a resource-based view will most likely describe their competitive advantage as owning unique 'resources'/core competencies. With slight exaggeration, one could say that this type of company demands that customers adapt to its offerings. This will for example be the case in markets where one can speak of a technology push. In Figure 9.2, we have summarized the terms used in marketing and strategic management that are used to indicate two different business orientations.

The question that has been left open so far is how the two types of business orientation that are summarized in Figure 9.2 relate to the Brand/Image Grid. The outside-in value orientation is most likely to be found at companies that attach more value to their *external* brand image than their internal brand image. The outside-in value orientation thus closely resembles the position that Show Brands take in the Brand/Image Grid. The inside-out value orientation, on the other hand, is most likely to be found at companies that do not focus on a strong *external* brand image, but do focus on product quality and attaining unique resources (like highly qualified employees). In other words, the inside-out value orientation closely resembles the position of Nerd Brands in the Brand/Image Grid.

The assumption underlying the dichotomy of market vs. product orientation is that a market-oriented company is on average more successful (ie profitable) than a product-oriented company. De Wit and Meyer (2014), however, regard the tension between the market- and resource-based views as a paradox, or in more philosophical terms as a 'Hegelian dialectic tension' between a thesis and an antithesis, which can only be solved through finding or formulating a synthesis (containing the best of 'both worlds'). So although in marketing and strategic management almost the same dichotomy is used to indicate two types of business orientation, the way academics deal with these dichotomies is quite different.

On the basis of the Brand/Image Grid and both dichotomies described above, we developed the Brand/Reputation Grid. The Brand/Reputation Grid builds further upon the Brand/Image Grid by relating the business focus of an organization to its external brand/ reputation.

The Brand/Reputation Grid

The Brand/Reputation Grid is built upon the idea that the prevalent business focus of a company not only has a strong influence on its internal culture, but also on how external stakeholders perceive the company brand.[6] Therefore, in the Brand/Reputation Grid we centre on the business/management focus and its effect on the internal and external perception of the brand. In the Brand/ Reputation Grid, two dimensions are plotted against each other: management style and communication style. Both dimensions are derived from the Competing Values Framework of Quinn and Rohrbaugh (1983). For both dimensions two values are distinguished:

- Management style may vary from focusing on 'control and stability' to 'flexibility and adaptability'.

- Communication style may vary from 'introvert and closed' to 'extrovert and open'.

The Brand/Reputation Grid is depicted in Figure 9.3. On the basis of the two dimensions, here also four types of organizations are distinguished: those with a focus on a product, a market, a process or a concept focus.

Below, we describe each of the business focuses of the Brand/ Reputation Grid on the basis of five characteristics. Four of these

Figure 9.3   The Brand/Reputation Grid with four different types of business/
management focus

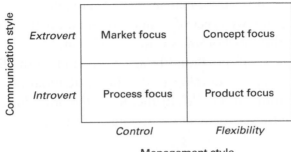

characteristics are derived from other, similar models or theoretical concepts; we have filled in one characteristic by logical reasoning:

1 Core competencies: an organization's raison d'être is often based on something it is good at: its core competencies (Hamel and Prahalad, 1994). These may differ between organizations with a product, market, process or concept focus.

2 Subject focus: does the management board focus on people or 'things'? And, if they focus on people, is the focus on their 'own' people (ie employees) or on third parties like customers and competitors? Insights on 'subject focus' are derived from the work of Coppenhagen (2002) who distinguishes between an 'I', 'they', 'it' and 'we' focus.

3 Culture: how can the corporate culture of the organization in question be described, and how do people treat each other within the company? Here we rely on the work of Cameron and Quinn (2012).

4 Values: what values are being pursued in the organization, both internally externally?

5 Brand role: what role is ascribed to the brand? What should it contribute to? Here we will refer to the work of Gromark *et al.* (2005) and Gromark and Melin (2011) on the brand orientation index.

Below we will describe each type of organization of the Brand/
Reputation Grid in more detail, by focusing on the above-mentioned five characteristics.

Companies with a process focus

A process-oriented organization places an emphasis on the best possible management of its processes (operational excellence). Core competencies often lie in the domains of *internal* and *external logistics*. This orientation can be seen at haulage or transport companies, where the focus is on timeliness, and at low-cost companies whose success is built on the efficiency of their processes. Here the organization tries to harmonize all business operations to such an extent that downtime or waste is limited to an absolute minimum. Although every single organization should try to optimize its processes, this does not mean this orientation always prevails. When something goes wrong at a Toyota plant in Japan, for example, the production line will be shut down if need be (by pulling the so-called Andon cord), in order to eradicate the problem once and for all. But still, you cannot say Toyota is primarily a process-oriented company (remember the four Ps of Toyota, mentioned at the start of this chapter).

Process-oriented organizations are also referred to as *It organizations*. The word 'it' refers to material matters here, such as systems, procedures, and premises. Instead of people, this type of organization's focus is mainly on things and procedures.

Cameron and Quinn (2012) describe companies with a process focus as organizations with a rigidly managed *formal culture*, in that employees' internal and external behaviour is regulated by formal processes. Relations between employees are defined by the terms 'superior' and 'inferior' (subordinate). You could also refer to this corporate culture as a 'functional hierarchy', with people placed in fixed roles that are firmly laid down in job descriptions, and with people getting a promotion – or a raise – if they meet certain functional requirements (such as through a system of periodical salary increments). Most processes in the organization are standardized or regulated. Important characteristics are structure, procedures, formal rules, efficiency, reliable delivery and cost containment. Leaders act as coordinators and organizers. There are also downsides to this type of working culture, namely the fact that employees are not encouraged to bring up improvement points, and are hardly stimulated to adopt a customer-driven attitude in their thinking and actions. With some exaggeration, you could say that employees at these kinds of organizations are after security, ie they work so as to provide for their living.

Companies with a process focus will most likely *not have defined any brand values* (due to the fact that there has been no brand development). In terms of the brand orientation index, the brand is almost non-existent or limited to having a logo (in the brand orientation index, this type of organization is referred to as *Sceptic*, ie *sceptical* towards brand management). Accordingly, there is unlikely to be a brand philosophy. In terms of the Brand/Image Grid, the brand of a company with a process focus can most likely be classified as a *Blank Brand*.

Companies with a market focus

A market-oriented organization is driven by the opportunities and chances offered by a market. Market-oriented companies are often very good at listening to the customer. This is expressed in the fact that they tend to have great quantities of market research done to stay abreast of what (potential) customers want. Market-oriented companies mostly start out by scouting out the market, mapping customer needs, and then looking how to produce the desired product. In terms of core competencies, these organizations are good at *collecting and interpreting the needs and desires of customers*, and at *responding to these needs and desires*. In doing so, they often try to beat the competition. Some market-driven companies go too far in their market orientation in that they become too preoccupied with (beating) their competitors. When that happens, the customer tends to lose out. In our opinion, a market orientation should never have such a strong competitive focus that it is at the expense of the customer. A market-oriented organization is also referred to as a *They organization*; their primarily focus lies on others – customers and/or competitors.

The literature on strategic management refers to market-oriented organizations as 'outside-in companies'. These are companies that tailor their products to the wishes of the market to the greatest possible degree. Their objective is acquiring a sizeable market share by giving the brand the best possible market position. Concepts such as benchmarking (comparing yourself to top performers in your market) and customer-value analysis (calculating or assessing the turnover that will be generated by a customer) are widely used at this kind of company.

Cameron and Quinn (2012) describe the culture of market-oriented organizations as a *performance culture*. This kind of organization has, just like an organization with a formal culture, a hierarchical setup. Employees at these companies are explicitly held responsible for their performance and behaviour. Market-oriented companies keep close tabs on their competitors, and have a strong drive to outperform them. Internally, these kinds of companies are also marked by ruthless competition, which is often reflected in the 'up or out' principle in their promotion policy (you either move up or move out; there is no room for stagnation). This is a culture that makes great demands on people. Aggression and a strong will to win are basic characteristics of a performance-driven corporate culture. Leaders assume a no-nonsense approach to management, and errors often lead to the rolling of heads. The problem with a performance culture is that it can backfire and lead to a certain degree of passivity (lethargy) and even absenteeism. In a performance culture, employees will be less likely to take the initiative to correct flaws in the organization.

The brand values within companies with a market focus will most likely be tuned to prevailing *customer values*. In terms of the brand orientation index, the brand is primarily used as a sales instrument, meant to convince customers of the 'greatness' of the product or service (in the brand orientation index, this type of company is referred to as *Salesmen*). Here the internal role of the brand is hardly or not recognized and the brand philosophy is used primarily to align employees with the external brand promise. This is what one may refer to as 'selling the brand inside' (Mitchell, 2002). In terms of the Brand/Image Grid, the brand of a company with a market focus can be best classified as a *Show Brand*.

Companies with a product focus

A product-oriented organization bases its marketing efforts on the old adage, 'a good product sells itself'. Product-oriented companies are often good at coming up with and making good-quality products.

Core competencies can usually be found in the domains of *production*, *quality performance* and *innovation*. Staff at this kind of company mostly consider professional skills and craftsmanship of paramount importance, which goes hand in hand with a high level of education among the workforce. Here an individual's knowledge and experience are essential to realizing a competitive edge, which is why we can refer to these companies as *I organizations*. Examples are companies where technology and/or innovations play an important role, such as ICT companies and fresh produce companies. Such companies often struggle when it comes to extolling the virtues of their brand; product features are often accentuated too much, whereas the benefits they offer customers or emotional purchase motivations are seriously underexposed.

Earlier we elaborated on the literature on strategic management, which describes these product-oriented organizations as companies that operate with a resource-based view, meaning they try to stand out in the market by having unique sources or competencies, such as specific know-how. With some exaggeration, you could say that following the resource-based view, companies expect the market to adapt to them. This is reflected in another popular adage, 'supply creates its own demand'. Inside-out companies often fail to properly monitor their competitors; benchmarking is hardly an issue at these companies. In extreme situations, customers are seen as a 'necessary evil', simply necessary to generate revenue.

Cameron and Quinn (2012) describe companies with a product focus as those that have a *family-like culture*. An organization with a family culture aims to create and uphold good internal relations, employee care and (individual) flexibility. But a side effect of such a setup is that individuals are hardly held accountable for errors; slip-ups are often glossed over because people shy away from confrontation. Employee loyalty, on the other hand, is relatively high. Employees generally have a job for life at organizations like these. Staff turnover is very low here; 20 or 30 years of service is unexceptional. In organizations with a family-like culture, leaders are often mentors (or even a 'father figure') to their staff members. The downside of this type of working culture is that engagements are not always kept, and that the organization is made up of so-called

'islands' or 'silos' – departments that operate more or less autono-
mously, without effective collaboration between them.

Companies with a product focus often have defined brand values
that largely overlap with organizational culture or *employee values*.
In terms of the brand orientation index, the brand will mainly serve
as an instrument or philosophy that describes 'how things are done',
internally. As the management style is not characterized by control
but by flexibility, employees are empowered to influence the role of
the brand. In the brand orientation index, this type of company is
referred to as *Educators*. In terms of the Brand/Image Grid, the brand
of a company with a product focus can be classified as a *Nerd Brand*.

Companies with a concept focus

A concept-oriented organization primarily focuses on motivating
its staff and optimizing collaboration between employees. This kind
of organization often gives its employees a large degree of freedom
(through trust), but equally expects top performance in return. Core
competencies can be described as being able to *motivate employees*
(turning them into brand ambassadors) and to have employees really
work together. This type of company is also referred to as a *We organization*; their primary focus is on employees and (strategic) partners.[7]
Many concept-oriented organizations do not have a separate brand
policy or marketing department; staff members at such organizations
are generally marked by a strong customer-focused attitude. CEOs of
this kind of company tend to focus on what Collins and Porras (1997)
refer to as 'clock building' instead of 'time telling', meaning that they
focus on building a company like clockwork, which will go on even
after they have left (Collins and Porras refer to charismatic leaders that
focus on short-term successes as 'time tellers'). It should be remembered here that a concept-oriented organization is far from closed to
the outside world, despite its unflinching culture. This kind of company
is often very alert to customer queries and does not hesitate to take
immediate action when faced with adverse publicity. In addition,
these kinds of organizations are very keen to strike partnerships with
other parties. Starbucks, for example, was at one point accused of not
paying a fair price to third-world coffee farmers, to which the company

retaliated by setting up the Care programme for these farmers (Schultz and Yong, 1997). The openness of this company is also reflected in the partnerships it has struck up with other parties, most notably United Airlines, which serves Starbucks coffee on its planes, and Barnes & Noble, where you can sip a Starbuck latte whilst browsing books.

Cameron and Quinn (2012) refer to organizations with a concept focus as characterized by an *adhocracy*.[8] The internal culture is highly dynamic and flexible, and its orientation is generally towards organizational excellence. In an adhocracy, work is mainly done on a project basis, with decisions made with an eye to optimizing the execution conditions for the project (not obstructed by any bureaucratic rules or personal goals). An adhocracy is therefore highly flexible and dynamic, and has a true entrepreneurial spirit. Individual interests play second fiddle to group interests; the emphasis is on teamwork, consensus and participation. This translates into low levels of absenteeism (remember the drop in absenteeism in the Nummi case), low staff turnover and exceptionally high levels of dedication in staff. Employees are, in other words, extremely committed to the company. This kind of organization is often seen as 'different', something people at the organization itself often take great pride in (such as at Southwest Airlines; see Miles and Mangold, 2005). Leaders in this kind of organization are characterized by an entrepreneurial spirit, an innovative attitude and a willingness to take risks. The downside is that an employee will have to adapt to the organization if they want to keep their job. The distinct culture at an adhocracy often leaves little room for employees who are unwilling to conform to the culture.

The brand values of companies with a concept focus will most likely be a mix of *customer, employee* and *societal-relevant values*. In terms of the brand orientation index, the brand is used as the business driver, and forms the *hub of all operations*. Where in many companies branding is subordinate to marketing, here one may conclude that it is the other way around. Branding – or the branding philosophy – has its influence on all departments within the company, whether it be marketing, procurement, production, sales or HRM. It is the brand philosophy (ie the concept) that determines how decisions are made. In terms of the Brand/Image Grid, the brand of a company with a concept focus can be classified as a *Personality Brand*.

Closing remarks on the Brand/Reputation Grid typology

Although the described characteristics apply to organizations to varying degrees, every organization will, in principle, have one dominant business focus and culture type. Unilever, for example, has a performance culture with a strong focus on its external image and the turnover generated by the individual product brands, even if there are elements of other cultural types within the organization. Most state services are characterized by a formal culture where controlled processing of information is key. Employees at KLM Airlines (part of Air France KLM) are highly loyal towards their employer and call themselves 'blue' after the dominant colour in the KLM logo and house style. This indicates a strong family culture at KLM. Google stimulates individuality and entrepreneurship, with employees working in project teams without a fixed hierarchy, which is a common feature in adhocracy. In Figure 9.4 we have summarized the findings on the Brand/Reputation Grid.

Figure 9.4 Summary of characteristics of the four types of organizations of the Brand/Reputation Grid

	Extrovert	
	Market focus	**Concept focus**
Control	• 'they' orientation • core competencies: market know-how, customer contact • performance culture • brand values = customer values • brand role = sales instrument	• 'we' orientation • core competencies: motivating employees, collaboration • adhocracy • brand values = combination of customer, employee and societal values • brand role = central hub
	Process focus	**Product focus**
	• 'it' orientation • core competencies: internal and external logistics • formal culture • brand values are not defined • brand role = logo	• 'I' orientation • core competencies: invent, production • family-like culture • brand values = employee values • brand role = product philosophy
	Introvert	

(Left axis: Control · Right axis: Flexibility)

In the first paragraph of this chapter, we introduced the term *living brands*. The sharp reader may have noticed that organizations with a concept focus fulfil the characteristics of a living brand. From a branding perspective, it is desirable to transform a process, market or product focus into a concept focus. Not only do organizations with a concept focus have a better brand image, brand orientation research also suggests they outperform the other three types of organization in terms of profits (Gromark *et al.*, 2005).[9] Previously, we noted that in marketing science a market orientation is seen as preferable to a product orientation. In strategic management, however, the tension between the market- and resource-based views is seen as a paradox that can only be solved through finding or formulating a synthesis (containing the best of 'both worlds'). On the basis of the Brand/ Reputation Grid, one might assume that a concept focus can be seen as the synthesis. And in marketing management, some authors have already argued that the distinction in market- and product-oriented companies is not sufficient enough to classify all kinds of companies (see for example, Grinstein, 2008).

Conclusion

In corporate branding, it is important to know whether you are dealing with a company with a process, product, market, or concept orientation. The business orientation may, for example, to a large degree determine what adversity you will encounter in building your brand. With some level of exaggeration, you could say that market-oriented companies will not easily receive broad internal support when stressing product features, and that board managers at product-oriented companies will not easily appreciate immaterial benefits in external communications. So, the first lesson of this chapter is to determine what kind of company you are.

The second lesson is that the key to successful branding is to a large degree dependent on organizational change (assuming the company in question is not concept oriented). Each type of organization (process, market, or product oriented) will face a different transformation process in becoming a concept-oriented organization. Below are some general principles for companies with either a process, market or product focus that want to transform themselves into a company with a concept focus:

- Companies with a *process* focus first need to work out their brand philosophy. They need to define a brand identity (what the brand should stand for, both for employees and customers), formalize the brand within the organization (in terms of functions and responsibilities), set budgets and targets, establish what difference the brand can make towards customers and employees (in terms of experience) and develop an execution plan to bring the brand to life.

- Companies with a *market* focus should redefine their brand thoroughly, involving their employees. The danger is that this will be initiated from the top down, as this way of working and thinking is embodied in the performance culture of these companies. Changes in brand policy should go hand in hand with a (bottom-up) culture change by empowering employees and 'letting go of control' by the management board. A fine example is given by Samuel Palmisano, who, in 2002, started a bottom-up reinvention of IBM's core values (Palmisano *et al.*, 2004). Companies with a market focus should thus strengthen their 'internal force'.

- Companies with a *product* focus should seek ways to 'involve the external world' into their brand. This can be done by meeting customers and trade partners and by talking to opinion leaders. Then managers need to look at working processes to make the company more sensitive to its market (customers and competitors). Besides this, pride amongst employees may be increased by an external campaign, showing the strengths of the company (or its products/services). Companies with a product focus can thus strengthen their 'external position' (which – as we explained before – may have a positive effect on the pride and motivation of employees).

How to initiate change around a shift in business focus is described by Gebhardt *et al.* (2006). These authors studied change processes of product-oriented companies, and on the basis of this they set up a four-stage process of change. Although this process was administered for product-oriented companies that turned themselves into market-oriented companies, this process may also work out for other types of change in business focus. Gebhardt *et al.* suggested the following four phases:

1 Initiation: in this phase, a small coalition of board members and/or employees recognizes that the current business focus will not lead to substantial growth of the company, or will bring the company severe problems. Often this recognition emerges from an external threat. Due to this, the coalition prepares a transformation process.

2 Reconstruction: in this phase, the coalition unveils its plan to the rest of the organization and tries to get 'all the people on the bus' who are convinced that a change is needed. Subsequently, the coalition will set out new values and norms and it will try to reconnect the company with the market (teams of employees meet with customers, trade agents and influencers in the market). In this phase, dissenters will leave (whether or not voluntary) and new 'believers' are hired. Finally, together with clients, employees experiment with a new way of working on projects.

3 Institutionalization: in this phase, changes are formalized and institutionalized. Rewards (in terms of salaries and job positions) are aligned to motivation and performance. Furthermore, employees are constantly made aware of the new values and norms, so that (parts of) the organization do not slip back into their old behaviours. An important thing to realize is that – at this stage – the power should shift from a mere top-down approach to one that is characterized by empowerment.

4 Maintenance: in this phase, the change – and the reasons for change – are remembered on a systematic basis. Think for example of culture maintenance rituals and regular initiatives for market connections.

Marketing – and to some degree branding – used to be professions that were very much outside-in oriented. In the last decade, many publications have appeared that stress an inside-out approach. In branding, it is now widely recognized that next to customers, employees should not only be seen as the receivers of internal brand communications, but also as the ones that strongly determine how the brand is perceived externally. This idea is very well understood, as illustrated by Ton (2014), who – in her book *The Good Jobs Strategy* – sets out the importance for a 'branding inside out' approach for retailers. Hopefully this chapter will encourage more authors to focus on the importance of this approach.

Endnotes

1 Pfeffer (1995) identified 13 practices for managing people:
(1) employment security; (2) selectivity in recruiting; (3) high wages;
(4) incentive pay; (5) employee ownership; (6) information sharing;
(7) participation and empowerment; (8) self-managed teams;
(9) training and skill development; (10) cross-utilization and cross-training; (11) symbolic egalitarianism (ie one cafeteria for all employees); (12) wage compression; (13) promotion from within.

2 Nowadays this facility is known for the production of Tesla cars.

3 The other three Ps are: (1) Problem solving (continuous improvement and learning); (2) Process (eliminate waste); and (3) Philosophy (long-term thinking).

4 The choice of the term 'Living Brands' was inspired by Nicholas Ind's book *Living the Brand* (2007; the first edition appeared in 2001) and the *Harvard Business Review* article 'Creating the Living Brand', written by Bendapudi and Bendapudi (2005).

5 We use the term 'brand reputation' to refer to the value that a brand may have for certain stakeholders. We explicitly choose 'reputation' here instead of 'image' because the term *reputation* signals a certain value (in terms of preferable vs. non-preferable).

6 The Brand/Reputation Grid was originally used as an exploration tool for corporate identity in positioning brands (see Riezebos and Van der Grinten, 2012).

7 Carr and Walton (2014) show that employees can already be motivated by merely stressing that they are working *together* on a job or assignment.

8 The term 'adhocracy' is a contraction of the Latin words 'ad hoc' (for a specific case) and the suffix '-cracy' (as in 'democracy') which comes from the Greek word 'kratein' (have the power, rule). Adhocracy literally means that decisions are made on the basis of arguments that are relevant to the matter at hand, and not on the basis of general organization-wide arguments and rules (such as in a bureaucracy).

9 In a study amongst 263 Swedish companies, Gromark *et al.* (2005) report average ebita figures (earnings before interest, taxes, and amortization) for companies with a process focus (which they have labelled as 'Sceptics') 8 per cent; for those with a market focus ('Salesmen') 9.6 per cent; those with a product focus ('Educators') 11.3 per cent; and for organizations with a concept focus ('Leaders') 14.4 per cent.

References

Bendapudi, N and Bendapudi, V (2005) Creating the living brand, *Harvard Business Review*, **83** (5), pp. 124–32

Bock, L (2015) *Work rules!: Insights from inside Google that will transform how you live and lead*, New York: Twelve, Hachette Book Group

Cameron, K S and Quinn, R E (1999; 2012), *Diagnosing and Changing Organizational Culture (based on the competing values framework)*, Reading, MA: Addison-Wesley

Carr, P B and Walton, G M (2014) Cues of working together fuel intrinsic motivation, *Journal of Experimental Social Psychology*, **53**, pp. 169–84

Catmull, E (2008) How Pixar fosters collective creativity, *Harvard Business Review*, **86**, (9), pp. 64–72

Collins, J C and Porras, J I (1997) *Built to Last: Successful habits of visionary companies*, New York: Harper Business

Coppenhagen, R (2002) *Creatieregie: Visie & verbinding bij verandering* (Controlling creation) Scriptum Management (publication in Dutch)

De Wit, B and Meyer, R (2014) *Strategy Synthesis: Managing strategy paradoxes to create competitive advantage*, Hampshire, UK: Cengage Learning EMEA

Freiberg, K and Freiberg, J (1997) *Nuts! Southwest Airlines' crazy recipe for business and personal success*, New York: Broadway Books

Gebhardt, G F, Carpenter, G S and Sherry, J F (2006) Creating a market orientation: A longitudinal, multiform, grounded analysis of cultural transformation, *Journal of Marketing*, **70** (4), pp. 37–55

Grinstein, A (2008) The relationships between market orientation and alternative strategic orientations: A meta-analysis, *European Journal of Marketing*, **42** (1/2), p. 115–34

Gromark, J, Astvik, T B and Melin, F (2005) *The Underlying Dimensions of Brand Orientation Index: A research project on brand orientation and profitablity in Sweden's 500 largest companies*, Sweden: Ruter Media Group AB

Gromark, J and Melin, F (2011) The underlying dimensions of brand orientation and its impact on financial performance, *Journal of Brand Management*, **18** (6), pp. 1–17

Hamel, G and Prahalad, C K (1994) *Competing for the Future: Breakthrough strategies for seizing control of your industry and creating the markets of tomorrow*, Boston, MA: Harvard Business School Press

Hsieh, T (2013) *Delivering Happiness: A path to profits, passion, and purpose*, New York: Grand Central Publishing

Ind, N (2007) *Living the Brand: How to transform every member of your organization into a brand champion,* London: Kogan Page

Kohli, A K and Jaworski, B J (1990) Market orientation: The construct, research propositions, and managerial implications, *Journal of Marketing*, **54** (2), pp. 1–18

Liker, J K (2004) *The Toyota Way: 14 management principles from the world's greatest manufacturer,* New York: McGraw-Hill

Liker, J K and Meier, D (2006) *The Toyota Way: Field book: A practical guide for implementing Toyota's 4Ps,* New York: McGraw-Hill

Liker, J K and Hoseus, M (2008), *Toyota culture: the heart and soul of the Toyota way.* New York: McGraw-Hill

Miles, S J and Mangold, W G (2005) Positioning Southwest Airlines through employee branding, *Business Horizons*, **48**, p. 535–45

Mitchell, C (2002) Selling the brand inside: You tell customers what makes you great. Do your employees know? *Harvard Business Review*, **80** (1), pp. 99–105

Morhart, F M, Herzog, W and Tomczak, T (2009) Brand-specific leadership: Turning employees into brand champions, *Journal of Marketing*, **73** (5), p. 122–42

Narver, J C and Slater, S F (1990) The effect of a market orientation on business profitability, *Journal of Marketing*, **54** (4), pp. 20–34

Palmisano, S J, Hemp, P and Stewart, T A (2004) Leading change when business is good, *Harvard Business Review*, **82** (12), pp. 60–70

Peters, T J and Waterman, R H Jr. (1982) *In Search of Excellence: Lessons from America's best-run companies,* London: Harper Business

Pfeffer, J (1995) Producing sustainable competitive advantage through the effective management of people, *Academy of Management Executive*, **9** (1), pp.95–106

Porter, M E (1985) *Competitive Advantage: Creating and sustaining superior performance*, New York: The Free Press

Quinn, R E and Rohrbaugh, J (1983) Spatial model of effectiveness criteria: Towards a competing values approach to organizational analysis, *Management Science*, **29** (3), pp. 363–77

Riezebos, R (2001) Internal Branding: Medewerkers zijn het merk (Internal branding: employees are the brand) *Tijdschrift voor Marketing*, **36** (6), pp. 24–26 (publication in Dutch)

Riezebos, R and Grinten, J van der (2012) *Positioning the Brand: An inside-out approach*, Abingdon, UK: Routledge

Schultz, H and Yong, D J (1997) *Pour Your Heart into It: How Starbucks built a company one cup at a time*, New York: Hyperion

Schultz, H and Gordon, J (2012) *Onward: How Starbucks fought for its life without losing its soul,* New York: Rodale Books

Ton, Z (2014) *The Good Jobs Strategy: How the smartest companies invest in employees to lower costs and boost profits*, New York: Houghton Mifflin Harcourt

Van Dyck, F (2016) *The longevity of brands (an interdisciplinary study based on Talcott Parson's AGIL-paradigm and its implications for strategic brand management (case study: the Apple brand),*dissertation, University of Brussels, Faculty of Economic and Social Sciences & Solvay Business School

How adidas attracts and retains talent

10

STEVE FOGARTY

The moment we knew we had created something new in employer branding was when one of our recruiters called and asked me to shut the 'Yeezy' recruitment campaign down. They couldn't manage the volume of candidates hitting them in such a short period of time. Within one hour of the campaign going live on our career site we had 1,300 candidates who had applied for the job.

Now your first reaction may be, well sure, you're adidas. But it would be a mistake to look at it that way. I can assure you that when I started with adidas over ten years ago we weren't on the map from a true 'talent' perspective. In fact I was sceptical about joining at the time because it seemed like a closed environment. I noticed a lot of turnover of HR staff and the recruiting was archaic. The reality is that we relied solely on our consumer brand to attract talent at that time, and most of the talent only came from our direct competitors. The brand was struggling to keep up with the competition, especially in the United States, and we were stepping into new territory, becoming a retailer as well as a wholesaler and an ecommerce operator. The marketplace in general was getting much smarter at attracting talent; we needed to get back in the game.

Prior to joining I spent seven and a half years at a strategic communications agency with a focus on the tech industry, called Waggener Edstrom. Pam Edstrom, one of the founders, had been Bill Gates' first PR Director. The company exposed me to three things: early stage innovations before they hit the general public, a culture of risk taking and exploration, and the power of storytelling. I didn't realize how important these three things would become in my career until much later on. The learning there was unparalleled but probably the part that would later become one of the most powerful tools in our employer branding arsenal was the storytelling component. I remember one of Waggener Edstrom's leaders at the time saying, look, the reason we are here is to enable people to understand inventions and innovations that can save their lives and change the world. They went on to say that we see inventors and innovators all time who have amazing inventions but don't have the ability to communicate them in a way where people understand them. And if they can't get people to understand, then the inventions sit in their labs instead of out there in the world making an impact. That always stuck with me.

So fast forward to adidas. Given where I was and the state of talent at adidas, I was hesitant to join. So why did I? adidas is headquartered in Herzogenaurach in Germany, but is one of the most global companies you can think of. We have a presence in almost every part of the world. So the first thing that I noticed when I came in for my interview was how international it was. I thought that was pretty cool. The person heading HR at the time was German and he had a strong desire to change the game. He understood we had to change. When I outlined the challenges they were facing, he said, 'Exactly, this is why you should join us.' He said, 'it will be an open pallet for you. We want you to come in and change things. We want you to push the status quo.' There was also an American in Germany called Steve Bonomo, who had just accepted the role of Global Head of Talent Acquisition. At the time this was a funny role because he had no team. It was just him in Germany. Before moving to this role, Steve had been managing recruiting at TaylorMade Golf (a brand adidas had acquired). When adidas headquarters realized it needed to start taking recruiting seriously, Steve was one of the few people in the company who had the experience to lead an RFP (Request for Proposal) process for a new ATS (Applicant Tracking System). Following this project, they offered him the global role. At the time there were roughly 11 recruiters in the organization, mostly in the United States, and outside of this it was HR staff and external headhunters managing recruiting. For my final interview I talked to Steve. When I heard his passion for where he wanted to take the recruiting organization and he asked me to join him in doing this, I thought it was a monumental challenge. But what would it be like if we could achieve this with a sleeping giant brand like adidas? How incredible would that be? It's hard to believe that's where we were just eight years ago. We now have a global team of 150 recruiters worldwide, five regions, a Strategic Search team, a Talent Acquisition Futures team (the team that I lead), a robust and thriving talent culture and the brand IS ON FIRE!

Let's go back to 2007 when I started. People knew our product, knew our brand but they didn't know us. Many thought we were an American brand. Some knew about our German roots but truly didn't understand our global reach. Even inside the organization we didn't know quite who we were. With only a handful of recruiters worldwide, we literally had nowhere to go but up. It was a daunting task, but as we didn't know any better, we just started to dig in.

At first we were tactical, sorting out business hot spots. For example, when I arrived, recruiting design talent was a major challenge. Talent on the outside had no idea of the robust career you could have as a designer at adidas. I also noticed it was a very self-critical culture. It was a truly global company but with its German roots it had very much a mentality of 'build it well, but don't brag about it'. Having just coming from one of the top tech PR firms in the world I knew that over-communicating is always better than not communicating. We needed to quickly find that balance of opening our doors to the outside world, showing the great work our teams were doing, and showcasing the talent people would have the opportunity to work with.

Besides making operational changes, I proposed to our Global Head of Design at the time that we showcase our top designers and our design centres. We would activate this on a recruitment marketing microsite built specifically for designers and expose top design talent to our culture at adidas. While the concept of microsites is pretty old by now, at the time it was a relatively new tool in recruitment marketing. It was also something the business was hesitant to do, because of the 'build it well and don't brag' culture. But in the end everybody agreed that we needed to try something different. We built a site that was visually stunning and told the stories of our designers. The entire

Figure 10.1 adidas Design Studios career site

experience on the site was built for design talent. The results showed. Designers responded by saying they connected with the experience and felt like we were talking to them, and they responded by applying. We also opened up more opportunities to students, getting our designers in front of them and continuing to drive more of an open culture. We knew we had amazing stories and teams. We just needed to tell the story.

This was a quick win. But there was a much bigger challenge to solve. How do we tell the story about our culture and our talent across the adidas Group to top talent everywhere? I have to say that it was a process of constant learning – trial by fire. Even rolling out a small recruitment ad for our global operations team caused controversy because I built the ad to represent adidas, but was quickly informed that I needed to represent the adidas Group, which covered all of our brands: adidas, Reebok, CCM Hockey, TaylorMade Golf – the list went on. This was very complex territory to navigate, especially since the adidas Group didn't really have a brand design team like our individual brand teams had; it was seen to be the holding company, and at the time was brand-less. We had virtually no guidance on how to represent the adidas Group from a design and storytelling perspective.

So how do you drive a global employer brand strategy from scratch, with a few people who really had zero extra time to focus on anything but recruiting talent? We had to keep it precise. I am a big believer in looking outside the industry for answers. The HR space wasn't really doing much that was new at the time in employer branding. It was the same old ads, videos and career sites. Employee testimonials and people throwing balls over cube walls to convey

Figure 10.2 adidas group brands

the fun they were having while they typed away and then talked about their 'passion' for the brand. Remember that word, passion – the most over-used word in company culture during the early Gen X-er days.

I remember picking up a book called *Killer Brands* by Frank Lane. The book really resonated with me because it was a very pragmatic approach to building a killer brand. I wanted to go back to the basics. The bleeding edge part could wait until we were ready to activate our strategy. We needed to first know what we wanted to say to the world about us as a talent organization. The book homed in on three things:

1 Focus: decide what you want to stand for and then focus relentlessly on it.

2 Alignment: how do you ensure that everybody you need to help drive the strategy is on the same page, telling the same story, amplifying its effect?

3 Linkage: how do you ensure the marketing activation is unequivocally communicating the message you want, and is distinct from other brands? (Lane, 2007)

This felt like the right approach for us. We had to focus. We had no other choice with what we had to work with. But this was easier said than done when you start talking about a company with multiple iconic brands – all with a lot of personality which we didn't want to dilute with our message. So we searched for the one thing all of our cultures had in common. Then we decided on what I call the 'duh factor' – what's right in front of your face. Sport. We all had this in common. But not just sport. Rather the ability to shape the future through sport. Our story was different from those of our competition. Their approach was to put sport in a 'war' context: winners and losers. They marketed their athletes as demigods, untouchable by the average person. With our European roots we really had a team approach to sport, taking athletes off the pedestal for our consumers and making sport accessible to everybody, no matter what sport and no matter what part of the world. So through a bit of work we decided to focus on 'Shape the Future of Sport'. If you joined us this was the promise we could offer, no matter which part of the organization you joined. Looking back, the solution might seem obvious – but it was not easy getting buy-in. Everybody wanted their own departmental message. We knew though that the power of our employer brand relied on consistently telling our story around the world, and amplifying this through our teams. If we had a thousand messages we wouldn't have an employer brand. We attempted to educate our internal stakeholders by putting this all into a business context.

We said it's really no different than branding in general. Let's take the adidas brand as an example. What is the end goal? Again, if you put it into the context of the brand, global brand communications is focused on the long-term survival and next-generation consumer connection with our brand. How do they get the next generation of consumers connected to the brand? Similar to the employer brand team, how do we, from a broad perspective, keep the right talent engaged with us as an employer and how do we drive applicant numbers in general to our jobs? With different regions, business areas and specific jobs, how do you maintain the overall employer brand integrity and attract the next generation of applicants to functional areas and to specific jobs?

After launching the strategy to the organization we broke down our execution into three parts. The first was activating our strategy with our internal stakeholders worldwide. We designed our employer brand manifesto, a hardcopy book that we distributed around the world, accompanied by virtual and in-person trainings. We also started to develop standard tools that our recruiters could use to attract talent: copy documents, ad templates and recruitment marketing activation plans. And finally we created global activations. With 'Shape the Future of Sport' as our focus, we decided that the best way to showcase this was to show our employees interacting with our athletes. So we worked with our sports marketing teams to secure athletes from TaylorMade, Reebok and adidas and created an interactive 'flash' site that allowed the candidate to choose a path and be guided by our athletes and our employees working together.

The site was ahead of its time, fortunately and unfortunately. From an inspiration perspective it hit the mark, but it wasn't without issues. We were running a global site with layer upon layer of video to create the virtual interaction and unfortunately not all of our end users had high enough bandwidth to run this at the time, which caused problems in various parts of the world. This was not an ideal user experience. With employer branding, both the strategy and execution are very important. You can have the most brilliant strategy, the best ideas, but if the execution doesn't convey the same spirit then it won't matter how good the strategy is. That said, we were moving the needle with attracting better talent, faster, but many lessons were learned along the way which allowed us to get smarter.

Shortly after the launch I remember speaking at an ERE (Electronic Recruiting Exchange) conference. I was sharing insights from marketing and branding to the audience. Afterwards several people approached me and asked me what area of the business I worked in. I said HR, Talent Acquisition. They looked dumbfounded. They said they thought I had worked in marketing. They said my entire presentation was on marketing and they weren't sure how it related to HR or Talent Acquisition. It made me quickly realize how far we had to go as an industry. I continued travelling and speaking around the world on this subject and over time there were more agencies showing up at conferences, more 'aha' moments, more design thinkers appearing and slowly but surely I witnessed the industry catching up.

At that point, we hit the gas pedal and accelerated. Roughly four years ago I approached the leadership team and pitched two things: 1) driving an employer brand from a strategic level with standardized tools was antiquated and we needed real-time design creation; and 2) we needed to storytell. We should stay focused on a singular differentiator but also have supporting stories which would appeal to a more diverse talent audience.

As part of this I proposed bringing employer brand design in-house. Up to this point we had outsourced all employer brand design. By going in-house we could go beyond investing in toolkits, start investing in real-time execution of recruiting marketing materials, and have a team so grounded in storytelling, image, graphics, copy, and film that we could build more relevant campaigns, faster and cheaper, and reach a broader range of talent.

The second piece was to gain further insights from employees around the world on what the top employer attributes were and the stories behind them – we then refined these into the most powerful, resonant stories for our key audiences. At the time I was able to

Figure 10.3 Building the adidas employer brand

convince leadership to move forward with the storytelling approach but the concept of insourcing design wasn't accepted. The leaders didn't feel the executive leadership team would approve design headcount in HR given how foreign this concept would be in this function. Instead we looked at outsourcing this with a small group of designers that were also able to execute our storytelling and image/copy approach.

To deliver on storytelling we reached out to our recruiting team worldwide and asked them to connect with employees from various business units, demographics and levels of engagement. And then we sent these recruiters each a Flip Video and had them interview these employees. We asked some simple questions. Why did you join the adidas Group? What keeps you here? What are your most inspirational moments since joining? What perks do you like the best? What was your most emotional moment? What do you like best about your career here?

Going back to the execution of employer branding as a communications problem and not a business problem, we wanted to get the best stories about the organization and then look to amplify these. We ended up with roughly 500 stories that we started to cluster into themes and eventually broke these down into five key stories. All of these then were presented back to leadership for sign-off and finally designed into what we called our Employer Brand Manifesto. This was the bible for how to communicate the adidas Group as an employer. It included image and copy guides as well as filmmaking guidance that could be activated by our recruiting team globally. We also leveraged it to educate our external design partners on our approach to ensure we aligned our communications strategies. This was presented to our communications team so we could ensure that we were telling the strongest talent stories at the time across our corporate and media channels. Below are the five key stories we built our employer brand around, with the first being our core focus.

SPORTS
LIFESTYLE
United by sports and fitness and the possibility it unlocks.

GLOBE-TROTTER
CAREERS
Our careers at this truly global player know no boundaries.

ORIGINALITY
Authenticity comes in countless forms, and we respect and celebrate the range of our people in both what they do and how they do it.

TRUE
CRAFTSMANSHIP
We thrive on the challenge of constantly improving everything we do.

TRIBAL
MEMBERSHIP
We work with people from all over the world and immediately accept them as part of something greater.

These storytelling platforms unlocked the door for our recruitment marketing campaigns to reach a broader audience and allowed us to focus our efforts and harness the collective, global team to amplify our voice globally. Alongside this we worked with our recruiting organization to update all of our digital platforms with engaging content targeted at a much wider audience than in the past. We also leveraged this for our online storytelling across our social landscape. We built new, digital toolkits and got much faster at executing recruitment advertising. We also started to differentiate better the balance between global strategy, execution, and local activation. We quickly increased our understanding of what worked and what didn't. With the rise of analytics we were able to get insights into what resonated with our audience. All of this listening and learning was the precursor to our future.

Fast-forward to 2017. Remember the design team I mentioned that we wanted to bring in-house. It's here. Did storytelling work? It did. And did the focus on analytics and the art of balancing strategy, execution, and local activation pay off? Yes.

Once you learn to take smart risks, fail fast, measure everything, and unleash a global team, you can quickly accelerate the entire system. In 2015 we went through quite significant change, with new leaders, a new head of adidas brand, new head of HR and new leadership at our North America headquarters where I sit. I was flying back from Europe, following a global recruiting offsite, and talking with one of our recruiting leaders about my master plan to bring back our previous head of recruiting and to centralize recruiting worldwide, essentially building the best recruiting team in the world. And that I would lead Talent Acquisition Futures, the innovation and design thinking engine behind the team. And then we walked into our new Chief Human Resources Officer's office and put the plan in front of her. Within one month we were operational. We then locked ourselves in a room and built our vision to create *the* best team out there: five regions, an executive recruiting arm and Talent Acquisition Futures team. We would drive innovation within the Global Talent Organization by leading the digitization of the talent experience, designing and building digital and analytics solutions, developing an employer brand strategy and activation and using decision science.

Building an in-house design team allowed us to quickly spread design thinking throughout the organization. We learned a lot more about the intersection of story and design. We could start to see how stories could be told through visual communications. We also learned a lot more about which elements of design were costly and time consuming and which were fast and tactical. We also brought film making in-house. Our understanding of employer brands had really matured and now we had the talent and creative expertise to bring it to life.

The three focus areas within Talent Acquisition Futures also allowed us to work more like an agency inside. With Digital and Analytics sitting side by side with Employer Branding and Talent Experience, we could build more inspirational and utilitarian experiences for our audiences. Everything was accelerating and the business was evolving rapidly. Having the team that could tackle these three areas became a differentiator in engaging top talent across industries, demographics and crafts.

Our new head of adidas Brand stood up in front of the entire organization in 2015, held up the book *Creativity, Inc.* by Ed Catmull and asked everybody to read it. I couldn't put it down. We were taking a stand as an organization, to put creativity at the top. Our consumers and our talent are Creators. Creators don't want to be dictated to, they want to express themselves to the world through their uniqueness and creativity. We announced our new driving behaviours of Creativity, Collaboration and Confidence. We launched a business strategy around Speed, Key Cities and Open Source. We put the People strategy back where it belonged – owned by the business, not HR – and rebuilt the HR Strategy to engage our talent with four core focus areas: 'Meaningful Reasons to Join and Stay', 'Role Models Who Inspire Us', 'Bring Forward Fresh and Diverse Perspectives', and 'Creative Climate to Make a Difference'.

With all of this we knew it was also time to evolve our Employee Value Proposition (EVP). We realized we were missing the intersection between what we offered as an organization, and what the next generation of Creators wanted in their career. We had previously looked internally, but we needed to understand the next generation of Creators that would propel our brand forward – and how to engage them.

So we solicited the help of storytelling gurus. We look
things: 1) Who are these so-called 'Creators' and what ar
ing for? 2) How does our industry at large currently
audience? 3) What is the intersection of what we offer and what they
are looking for?

The other element was how to tie this directly to the new direction
of the organization to ensure the stories we were promoting about
adidas as an employer were inarguably true. What we found was
interesting.

First we needed to define what a Creator was. Ultimately what we
determined was that it could be anyone but what represented it best
were the entrepreneurial minded, creatives, innovators, disruptors
and collaborators. We captured this as follows.

> Creators can be found in every industry, in every type of job, in every
> country around the world. Creators find inspiration in unlikely places,
> they look at the world in their own unique way, and they have an uncanny
> ability to connect the dots that others just don't see. They are obsessed
> with a culture, environment and team that unleashes creative potential and
> gives all of us a chance to make a real impact. They want to build a better
> tomorrow.

From here we looked at what this archetype looks for in their career.
Here's what we captured.

> They are purpose driven.
> They prefer flat and bottom-up organizations.
> They want transparent, collaborative and open source environments.
> They have a love of the unknown.
> They crave clarity and simplicity.

Our research also suggested that as an industry we speak in clichés
and hyperboles, and that the industry is self-promoting.

We then looked to our strengths as an employer. We took our past research and the direction of the organization to ensure what we developed was properly anchored. From this we defined the new direction for the Employer Brand strategy and we built it.

We had enough insights. We went beyond just creating the stories that we wanted to tell. We also created the frame in which to tell these stories. Looking at our target audience, we wanted to ensure we were always telling the stories in the context of the future and to remind everyone that rather than dwelling on the past, every day is an opportunity to create. Of course, we know it's important to celebrate our heritage but we should do so in the context of how it helps us shape the future. If we talked about Adi Dassler, our founder, we would talk about him as a visionary. This is important. The stories in and of themselves are important, but there are many ways to tell stories. And the way we wanted to tell our story was in the context of the future. When we talk about the creator archetype, these are people who want to have the opportunity to create a better tomorrow.

The second thing we did was to ensure our stories were grounded in belief. Great stories always are. But the challenge is to not tell people what to believe; the art is to tell a story in a way where the person hearing it can form their own belief about the story. If it's done right the intended message will be engaging. With this we were ready to create our newest strategic framework for employer branding at the adidas Group. Our six beliefs:

THROUGH
SPORT,
WE HAVE
THE POWER
TO CHANGE
LIVES
Sport matters. It gets people off the couch and into the gym.
It fights disease, deepens friendships and improves lives.
It strengthens muscles, increases self-confidence and teaches lessons
that last a lifetime. Through sport, we have the power to change lives.

THE FUTURE
RUNS ON DIVERSE
AND FRESH
PERSPECTIVES

Adi Dassler looked at factory workers and saw athletes. He picked up army surplus canvas and saw track spikes. It's the people who see the world a little differently than the rest who create the breakthroughs that inspire us all. The more diverse perspectives and life experiences we support and encourage, the more often those breakthroughs will happen. At adidas Group, we seek people with different perspectives and life experiences and allow them to bring their true self to work every day. This isn't just a nicety. It's a business necessity.

CAREERS WITHOUT BORDERS

Exposing your talents to as many different cultures, languages, life experiences and points of view as possible is the fastest way to grow.

PIONEERING
THE FUTURE
OF WORK

Imagination, teamwork and the courage to share your ideas all need the right environment to thrive. Which is why we're focused on being at the epicentre of global culture and pioneering a future workplace that facilitates faster decision making, creative solutions and more opportunities for spontaneous collaboration.

SPORT
NEEDS
A PLACE

Sport needs a healthier, stronger, more sustainable and more socially responsible world. Changing the way an industry does business isn't quick or easy.
It's a marathon, not a sprint. Which is why we've made this a core priority for the entire adidas Group.

COLLABORATING
WITH THOSE WHO
INSPIRE US

We invite anyone and everyone whose curiosity and creativity inspires us to be part of our brands. We open our doors to collaborators from all walks of life, open our ears to their points of view, and are generous with our own insights and experience, so that we can all co-create the future together.

If you fast-forward back to today, we are on our way to building an agency within adidas, guided by one of our most impactful strategies yet. Our focus on Employer Brand Design, Digital and Analytics and Talent Experience have allowed us to take our story framework and execute this across our digital social and recruitment marketing channels worldwide. These stories are built into our Employer Brand Experience. This, coupled with our film, graphic design, copywriting and analytics expertise, has allowed us to scale across a broad spectrum of business demands at a global level, amplified by a team trained in employer brand activation and empowered to create.

We never rest. However, the strategy has paid off. We have witnessed nearly double the volume through our talent pipelines and have watched the quality of the talent increase. We are currently receiving roughly 8 million visitors to our career site per year, almost double since we introduced the new strategy and executed it. We have roughly 4 million job views, and approaching 800,000 applications for roughly 4–6,000 corporate roles a year. We are up in every category and all of this fuels roughly 60 per cent of our hires. We have seen our engagement levels go up across our social channels and we've seen the performance of our organization talent continue to rise.

Building an employer brand at one of the world's most iconic brands has been the ride of a lifetime. I've had the very fortunate honour to work with some of the most creative people in the industry, including our Talent Futures team, our creative partners and many adidas visionaries.

References

Catmull, E (2014) *Creativity, Inc.: Overcoming the unseen forces that stand in the way of true inspiration,* Random House
Lane, F (2007) *Killer Brands: Create and market a brand that will annihilate the competition,* Avon, MA: Adams Media

Internal brand management: employees as a target group for brand management

11

CHRISTOPH BURMANN AND RICO PIEHLER

Relevance of internal brand management

Brand management has mainly been applied to external stakeholders, such as customers, but the admittedly important development of, and communication about, the brand promise externally really represents only one side of the coin (Ind, 2003). The other side is the fulfilment of the brand promise, because only when customers experience this do they achieve satisfaction, brand trust, and stronger brand–customer relationships (Delgado-Ballester *et al.*, 2003; Burmann and Zeplin, 2005; Piehler *et al.*, 2015). As employees are directly or indirectly responsible for the fulfilment of the brand promise, so they represent an important, internal target for brand management efforts (Harris and de Chernatony, 2001; Mitchell, 2002; Ind, 2003). Consequently, as brand management research and practice has expanded in the past 15 years to include internal stakeholders such as employees, so internal brand management, or internal branding, has developed in organizational initiatives that address employees from a brand management perspective (Piehler *et al.*, 2016). The growing recognition that employees are a key source of sustainable differentiation and competitive advantage in markets for increasingly similar products and services (Mosley, 2007) means the relevance of internal brand management can only grow.

Current state of research

Piehler *et al.* (2015) define *internal brand management* (IBM) as a concept that implements the brand cognitively, affectively, and behaviourally at the employee level. This important management concept involves not just frontline employees but all employees in the organization. Customer-facing employees shape customers' experience of the brand directly, through their actions at brand touch points. Consequently, the relevance of IBM may be greater when employees are more prominently involved in the delivery of products and services, interact more directly with customers, or are more diverse. Those employees who do not face customers directly (eg R&D scientists, members of the manufacturing department) still shape the brand experience indirectly through their role as internal suppliers to customer-facing employees (eg responsible for product and service quality). A similar logic for an expanded view of IBM applies across hierarchical levels: IBM does not only represent an important management concept for employees in entry-level positions. Supervisors and managers contribute to the fulfilment of the brand promise through their brand-oriented leadership and implementation of structures and processes that support employees in entry-level positions (Piehler *et al.*, 2016). Due to the intangibility of services, IBM is particularly important for service brands, because customers often use employee behaviour as an indicator for their evaluations of service quality.

Early discussions of IBM started with Thomson *et al.* (1999), Ind (2001), Bergstrom *et al.* (2002), de Chernatony *et al.* (2003), and Ind (2003). Miles and Mangold (2004; 2005) and Burmann and Zeplin (2005) propose more comprehensive IBM models that include outcomes and managerial practices; these models have been validated empirically by Burmann *et al.* (2009) and Miles *et al.* (2011)

respectively. Similarly comprehensive IBM models were offered by Punjaisri *et al.* (2008; 2009), Punjaisri and Wilson (2011), Baumgarth and Schmidt (2010), and King and Grace (2010; 2012). Several studies focus on specific IBM outcomes or specific managerial practices that affect certain IBM outcomes. Therefore, the next sections detail some key IBM outcomes and managerial IBM practices that may affect these outcomes.

Internal brand management outcomes

Brand citizenship behaviour

Because IBM aims to align employee behaviour with the brand identity and promise, brand-related employee behaviours, such as brand-consistent behaviour (Henkel *et al.*, 2007), brand performance (Punjaisri and Wilson, 2011), brand-supporting/supportive behaviour (Vallaster and de Chernatony, 2005; Punjaisri *et al.*, 2008; King, 2010), employee brand equity (King *et al.*, 2012), brand-building behaviour (Morhart *et al.*, 2009; Löhndorf and Diamantopoulos, 2014), and brand citizenship behaviour (Burmann and Zeplin, 2005; King and Grace, 2010, 2012; Piehler *et al.*, 2015) are frequently proposed as important behavioural IBM outcomes. *Brand citizenship behaviour* (BCB) refers to employee behaviours 'that are consistent with the brand identity and brand promise such that together they strengthen the brand' (Piehler *et al.*, 2016, p. 1577); it is one of the most popular outcomes in prior literature, for four main reasons:

1 BCB was introduced by Burmann and Zeplin (2005) as one of the first constructs available to measure brand-related employee behaviour.

2 It is the basis for other kinds of brand-related behaviour, such as employee brand equity and brand-building behaviour.

3 BCB has a clear theoretical foundation in organizational behaviour literature and is adapted from organizational citizenship behaviour.

4 It is the most-often-used behavioural outcome in IBM literature.

Previous studies also support the relevance of brand-related employee behaviour such as BCB for external brand management objectives. Sirianni *et al.* (2013) empirically confirm that brand evaluation and customer-based brand equity tend to be more favourable when employee behaviour aligns with the brand's personality. Tuominen *et al.* (2016) empirically identify the positive effect of brand value adoption on brand performance. Using employee and management surveys, Baumgarth and Schmidt (2010) empirically validate the positive relationship between brand-related employee behaviours such as BCB and customer-based brand equity. Offering support for this finding with an employee survey and customer service ratings, Baker *et al.* (2014) empirically confirm that BCB positively affects service performance.

For the conceptualization of BCB, prior literature provides both unidimensional (King and Grace, 2010, 2012; Baker *et al.*, 2014) and multidimensional (Burmann and Zeplin, 2005; Burmann *et al.*, 2009; Shaari *et al.*, 2011; Chang *et al.*, 2012; Porricelli *et al.*, 2014; Nyadzayo *et al.*, 2015, 2016; Piehler *et al.*, 2015) versions. Piehler *et al.* (2016) argue that BCB should be conceptualized as multidimensional, to reflect the diverse employee behaviours required to strengthen the brand. Unfortunately though, the existing multidimensional conceptualizations differ in the number of dimensions they contain and their content. The following dimensions have been empirically validated in previous IBM research:

- Willingness to help (Burmann *et al.*, 2009), helping behaviour (Shaari *et al.*, 2011; Nyadzayo *et al.*, 2015, 2016), helping behaviours and brand consideration (Chang *et al.*, 2012), or brand acceptance (Porricelli *et al.*, 2014).

- Brand enthusiasm (Burmann *et al.*, 2009; Baumgarth and Schmidt, 2010; Nyadzayo *et al.*, 2015, 2016) or brand endorsement (Shaari *et al.*, 2011; Nyadzayo *et al.*, 2015, 2016; Piehler *et al.*, 2015, 2016).

- Willingness for further development (Burmann *et al.*, 2009), willingness to support brand development (Baumgarth and Schmidt, 2010), self–brand development (Shaari *et al.*, 2011), self-development of brand enhancement (Chang *et al.*, 2012), or brand development (Porricelli *et al.*, 2014; Piehler *et al.*, 2015, 2016).

- Sportsmanship (Shaari *et al.*, 2011) or brand sportsmanship (Chang *et al.*, 2012).

- Brand-consistent intra-role behaviour (Baumgarth and Schmidt, 2010) or brand compliance (Piehler *et al.*, 2015, 2016).

The helping dimension refers to a positive attitude, friendliness, helpfulness, and empathy toward internal and external customers, as well as taking responsibility for tasks outside of the employee's own area of responsibility, if necessary (Burmann and Zeplin, 2005). The brand enthusiasm/endorsement dimension represents the conscious espousal of, and advocacy for, the brand, including behaviours such as recommending the brand to potential employees and customers, representing the brand favourably, defending the brand, and passing on the brand identity to new employees (Burmann and Zeplin, 2005; Nyadzayo *et al.*, 2015, 2016, Piehler *et al.*, 2015, 2016). In the development dimension, the focal behaviours enhance employees' brand-related knowledge, skills, and abilities (Burmann and Zeplin, 2005; Chang *et al.*, 2012). It also includes behaviours that contribute to brand development, to improve customers' brand experience through the adaptation of the brand identity concept to changing market needs or new organizational competencies by sharing customer feedback or generating innovative ideas (Burmann and Zeplin, 2005; Piehler *et al.*, 2015, 2016). The (brand) sportsmanship dimension indicates that employees engage with the brand, even at high opportunity costs, and do not complain (Burmann and Zeplin, 2005). Finally, the brand compliance dimension refers to behaviours such as following brand-related rules and instructions to support branding objectives and avoid damaging the brand (Baumgarth and Schmidt, 2010; Piehler *et al.*, 2015, 2016).

For employees to engage in BCB, the brand must be implemented affectively and cognitively. Therefore, in IBM literature, brand commitment (Burmann and Zeplin, 2005; King and Grace, 2012) and brand identification (Piehler *et al.*, 2016) represent affective outcomes. Brand understanding (Xiong *et al.*, 2013; Piehler *et al.*, 2015, 2016), brand knowledge (Kimpakorn and Tocquer, 2009; Baumgarth and Schmidt, 2010; Löhndorf and Diamantopoulos,

2014; Dean *et al.*, 2016; Terglav *et al.*, 2016), or knowledge of the desired brand image (Miles and Mangold, 2005; Miles *et al.*, 2011) instead appear as cognitive outcomes.

Brand commitment

Burmann and Zeplin (2005, p. 284) define brand commitment generally as 'the extent of psychological attachment of employees to the brand'.' The conceptualization of this construct in IBM literature is not consistent though. For example, Burmann and Zeplin (2005) adapt an organizational commitment conceptualization from O'Reilly and Chatman (1986), using compliance, identification, and internalization as dimensions. Mahnert and Torres (2007) and Kimpakorn and Tocquer (2010) instead adapt unidimensional organizational commitment conceptualizations from Mowday *et al.* (1979) and Cook and Wall (1980), respectively. Most studies conceptualize brand commitment as an emotional attachment (Punjaisri *et al.*, 2009; Punjaisri and Wilson, 2007, 2011) or affective commitment (King, 2010; King and Grace 2010, 2012; Piehler *et al.*, 2015). By adapting the affective dimension of Allen and Meyer's (1990) three-component conceptualization of organizational commitment, Piehler *et al.* (2016, p. 1578) describe the *brand commitment* of employees as a 'unidimensional construct, reflecting an emotional attachment to the brand'. Employees with an emotional attachment to the brand should strengthen it through their behaviour. This relationship with BCB has been consistently validated (Burmann *et al.*, 2009; King and Grace, 2012; Piehler *et al.*, 2015, 2016).

Brand identification

Brand identification entails an employee's sense of belonging to the brand (Punjaisri and Wilson, 2011). Burmann and Zeplin (2005) regard brand identification as part of brand commitment, but IBM publications that acknowledge developments in organizational behaviour research (eg Gautam *et al.*, 2004; Ashforth *et al.*, 2008) view identification and commitment as related but separate constructs (Punjaisri *et al.*, 2009; Piehler *et al.*, 2016). Again, the conceptualization of brand identification is not consistent. Punjaisri *et al.* (2009) regard the construct as a cognitive–affective IBM outcome. Because cognitive identification precedes affective identification, and affective identification is a better predictor of employee commitment and behaviour (Johnson *et al.*, 2012), Piehler *et al.* (2016, p. 1579) suggest that brand identification is an affective IBM outcome, in which context they define *brand identification* as 'employees' feeling of belonging to the brand'.

Identification is a basis for commitment in a general model of commitment (Meyer and Herscovitch, 2001). Employees with positive feelings about belonging to the brand should grow more emotionally attached to it. Punjaisri *et al.* (2009) and Piehler *et al.* (2016) deliver empirical validation of this relationship in an IBM context. Brand identification is also an antecedent of brand-supporting employee behaviour (Punjaisri and Wilson, 2011) and BCB (Piehler *et al.*, 2016), as similarly deduced from organizational behaviour research that presents identification as an important antecedent of organizational citizenship behaviour (Johnson *et al.*, 2012). In line with social identity theory (Tajfel, 1978, 1982; Tajfel and Turner, 1986), employees who have positive feelings about belonging to the brand likely engage in in-role and extra-role behaviours to strengthen the brand. Löhndorf and Diamantopoulos (2014) and Piehler *et al.* (2016) deliver empirical support for this effect.

Brand understanding

Finally, brand understanding – also referred to as brand knowledge (Kimpakorn and Tocquer, 2009; Baumgarth and Schmidt, 2010; Löhndorf and Diamantopoulos, 2014; Dean *et al.*, 2016; Terglav *et al.*, 2016) or knowledge of the desired brand image (Miles and Mangold, 2005; Miles *et al.*, 2011) – represents an important cognitive IBM outcome (Xiong *et al.*, 2013; Piehler *et al.*, 2015). Piehler *et al.* (2016, p. 1580) define *brand understanding* as 'employees' comprehension of brand-related information'. For the conceptualization, prior literature again details both unidimensional (Kimpakorn and Tocquer, 2009; Baumgarth and Schmidt, 2010; Miles *et al.*, 2011; Löhndorf and Diamantopoulos, 2014; Terglav *et al.*, 2016) and multidimensional (Xiong *et al.*, 2013; Piehler *et al.*, 2015) options. However, a multidimensional perspective appears more appropriate for capturing the diverse brand-related information that employees are required to possess to develop positive feelings of belonging to the brand, to become attached to it, and to be able to deliver on the brand promise (Piehler *et al.*, 2016). Four dimensions of brand understanding emerge from prior IBM research:

- Brand relevance refers to employees' understanding that the brand is important for the organization's success, in that employees must perceive the brand as meaningful (Xiong *et al.*, 2013; Piehler *et al.*, 2015, 2016).

- Behaviour relevance reflects employees' realization that they contribute, with their behaviour, to the brand's perception and subsequent success (Kimpakorn and Tocquer, 2009; Xiong *et al.*, 2013; Piehler *et al.*, 2015, 2016).

- Brand knowledge represents employees' perceptions of what the brand represents, indicating that they have sufficient knowledge of the brand identity and promise (Kimpakorn and Tocquer, 2009; Baumgarth and Schmidt, 2010; Löhndorf and Diamantopoulos, 2014; Piehler *et al.*, 2015, 2016; Terglav *et al.*, 2016).

- Brand confidence reveals whether employees can confidently translate an abstract brand identity and brand promise into specific, brand-strengthening behaviours in their daily work (Baumgarth and Schmidt, 2010; Xiong *et al.*, 2013; Piehler *et al.*, 2015, 2016).

Brand understanding thus is an important antecedent of brand identification, brand commitment, and BCB. According to social identity theory, knowledge about group characteristics is necessary to enable group comparisons, so to identify with the brand, employees must have sufficient brand understanding; without it, they will not develop positive feelings about belonging to the brand (Piehler *et al.*, 2016). Löhndorf and Diamantopoulos (2014) and Piehler *et al.* (2016) deliver empirical validation of this effect. In addition, if employees lack appropriate brand understanding, they do not know how to perform their brand-related roles and experience role ambiguity (King and Grace, 2010), which then has a negative effect on commitment (Meyer *et al.*, 2002). Conversely, if employees have proper brand understanding, role clarity increases (King, 2010) and affects brand commitment positively (King *et al.*, 2012). Xiong *et al.* (2013), Piehler *et al.* (2015, 2016) and Terglav *et al.* (2016) offer empirical support for this relationship. Finally, without brand understanding, employees cannot behave in accordance with the brand's identity and promise. Role ambiguity also has negative effects on citizenship behaviours (Podsakoff *et al.*, 1996; Eatough *et al.*, 2011), so brand understanding is an important antecedent of BCB (Xiong *et al.*, 2013; Piehler *et al.*, 2015, 2016). With sufficient brand understanding, role clarity increases (King, 2010), which enhances BCB and related behaviours (King, 2010; King and Grace, 2010; King *et al.*, 2012). Empirically, Löhndorf and Diamantopoulos (2014) and Piehler *et al.* (2015, 2016) validate this relationship between brand understanding and BCB.

Figure 11.1 summarizes the four important IBM outcomes and their relationships.

Figure 11.1 Internal brand management outcomes

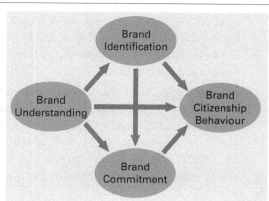

Managerial internal brand management practices

Overview

From a management perspective, it is important to understand how IBM outcomes might be affected by managerial practices, such as brand-oriented leadership, brand-oriented human resource management, and internal and external brand communication (Table 11.1).

Table 11.1 Managerial IBM practices in IBM literature

Managerial IBM practices	Sources in IBM literature
Brand-oriented Leadership	Miles and Mangold (2004; 2005); Burmann and Zeplin (2005); Vallaster and de Chernatony (2005); de Chernatony *et al.* (2006); Ind (2007); Burmann *et al.* (2009); Morhart *et al.* (2009); Miles *et al.* (2011); Merrilees and Frazer (2013); Porricelli *et al.* (2014); Piehler *et al.* (2015); Saleem and Iglesias (2016); Terglav *et al.* (2016)
Brand-oriented Human Resource Management	Miles and Mangold (2004; 2005); Aurand *et al.* (2005); Burmann and Zeplin (2005); de Chernatony *et al.* (2006); Ind (2007); Mahnert and Torres (2007); Punjaisri and Wilson (2007; 2011); Punjaisri *et al.* (2008; 2009); Burmann *et al.* (2009); M'zungu *et al.* (2010); Miles *et al.* (2011); Matanda and Ndubisi (2013); Piehler *et al.* (2015); Saleem and Iglesias (2016)
Internal Brand Communication	Thomson *et al.* (1999); Burmann and Zeplin (2005); Vallaster and de Chernatony (2005); de Chernatony *et al.* (2006); Ind (2007); Mahnert and Torres (2007); Punjaisri and Wilson (2007; 2011); Punjaisri *et al.* (2008; 2009); Burmann *et al.* (2009); Baker *et al.* (2014); Porricelli *et al.* (2014); du Preez and Bendixen (2015); Piehler *et al.* (2015); Saleem and Iglesias (2016)
External Brand Communication	Mitchell (2002); Miles and Mangold (2004, 2005); Burmann and Zeplin (2005); de Chernatony *et al.* (2006); Henkel *et al.* (2007); Ind (2007); Mahnert and Torres (2007); M'zungu *et al.* (2010); Wentzel *et al.* (2010); Miles *et al.* (2011); Hughes (2013); du Preez and Bendixen (2015); Piehler *et al.* (2015); Saleem and Iglesias (2016)

Brand-oriented leadership

Brand-oriented leadership can encompass brand-oriented transactional, transformational, and empowering forms of leadership. Burmann and Zeplin (2005) define *brand-oriented transactional leadership* as behaviours based on social exchange processes. Following Morhart *et al.* (2009), such behaviours include specifying behavioural standards for employees' roles as brand representatives and rewarding employees when expectations are met, and clarifying what constitutes undesired behaviours and punishing employees for not following specified standards. These behaviours represents a brand-specific adaptation of Bass's (1985) contingent reward and management-by-exception dimension.

In contrast, Burmann and Zeplin (2005, p. 293) define *brand-oriented transformational leadership* as behaviours 'that influence the value systems and aspirations of the individual members of the organization and induce them to transcend their own self-interests for the sake of the brand.' Similarly, Morhart *et al.* (2009, p. 123) describe brand-oriented transformational leadership as 'a leader's approach to motivating his or her followers to act on behalf of the corporate brand by appealing to their values and personal convictions'. Following Morhart *et al.* (2009), this form of leadership comprises behaviours such as acting like a role model and living the brand, articulating the brand vision and arousing employees' involvement and pride in the brand, encouraging employees to rethink their jobs from a branding perspective and supporting them in interpreting the brand promise and its implications for their daily work, and teaching and coaching employees to become brand representatives (see Chapter 3 by Felicitas Morhart in this book for pros and cons of this leadership style). Acting like a role model and living the brand is a brand-specific adaptation of Bass's (1985) charisma/idealized influence dimension (Morhart *et al.*, 2009); de Chernatony and Harris (2000) realize that managers' behaviours affect employees' perceptions and acceptance of the brand's identity. Burmann and Zeplin (2005) also highlight the role of management when they apply social learning theory (Bandura, 1977), such that people learn new attitudes and behaviours by observing the behaviours of other people. Consequently, management on the macro and micro levels should function like a role model (Burmann and Zeplin, 2005). Vallaster and de Chernatony (2005) and Ind (2007) argue that leaders must support and actively demonstrate commitment to the internal branding process while also acting as role models and living the brand in an authentic and honest rather than a forced or artificial way. De Chernatony *et al.* (2006) identify the behaviour of senior management and top management as important tools for communicating the brand to employees; their actions thus cannot contradict the brand's values. Through the mediating effect of relatedness to the brand community and role identity competence, autonomy, and internalization, Morhart *et al.* (2009) predict an effect of brand-oriented transformational leadership on in-role and extra-role brand-building behaviours. Terglav *et al.* (2016) consider this dimension of brand-oriented transformational leadership important, in that it affects brand knowledge and thus brand commitment of employees. Articulating the brand vision and arousing employees' involvement and pride represents a brand-specific adaptation of Bass's (1985) inspirational motivation dimension (Morhart *et al.*, 2009). According to Vallaster and de Chernatony (2005), an inspiring brand vision communicated in a top-down manner relates positively to employees' commitment and subsequent behaviour. Encouraging employees to rethink their jobs by taking a branding perspective and supporting employees to interpret the brand promise and its implications for their daily work is a brand-specific adaptation of Bass's (1985) intellectual stimulation dimension (Morhart *et al.*, 2009), in line with Vallaster and de Chernatony's (2005) postulation that leaders have an active role in translating the brand's promise into action. Finally, teaching and coaching employees to become brand representatives is a brand-specific version of Bass's (1985) individualized consideration dimension (Morhart *et al.*, 2009).

In addition to transactional and transformational leadership styles, *brand-oriented empowering leadership* can be an effective managerial IBM practice (Piehler *et al.*, 2015). This style aims to enhance employees' brand-oriented (psychological) empowerment, going beyond the structural empowerment usually detailed in IBM literature, which refers to the delegation of brand-related decision making from management to employees (Burmann and Zeplin, 2005; Mahnert and Torres, 2007; Morhart *et al.*, 2009). According to Konczak *et al.*'s (2000) Leader Empowering Behaviour Questionnaire (LEBQ) and Arnold *et al.*'s (2000) Empowering Leadership Questionnaire (ELQ), empowering leadership behaviours include leading by example, coaching, participative decision making, information sharing, showing concern and interacting with the team, delegating authority, being accountable, encouraging self-directed decisions, and developing skills.

Empirically, Burmann *et al.* (2009) confirm a positive effect of brand-oriented leadership that consists of role modelling by living the brand, brand-oriented transformational leadership, and empowerment on the brand commitment of employees. Through the mediating effect of relatedness to the brand community and role identity competence, autonomy, and internalization, Morhart *et al.* (2009) confirm that brand-oriented transformational leadership influences in-role and extra-role brand-building behaviours. They also reveal that moderately used, brand-oriented transactional leadership adds to the value of brand-oriented transformational leadership by strengthening its positive effects on follower outcomes. Miles *et al.* (2011) show empirically that manager behaviour that reflects the organization's values positively affects employees' perceived knowledge of the organization's desired brand. In addition, Porricelli *et al.* (2014) determine that brand leadership, adapted from Burmann *et al.* (2009), is part of an IBM practices construct that affects employees' brand commitment and BCB. According to Merrilees and Frazer (2013), the effect of brand commitment on franchisees' attitudes toward the franchisor brand is stronger for leaders who adopt a transformational leadership style. Finally, Terglav *et al.* (2016) empirically confirm that brand-oriented leadership affects employees' brand knowledge. It thus is no surprise that, in their literature analysis, Saleem and Iglesias (2016) identify brand-oriented leadership as an important dimension of internal branding. In summary, brand-oriented leadership is an important managerial IBM practice that influences the IBM outcomes of brand understanding, brand identification, brand commitment, and BCB.

Brand-oriented human resource management

Brand-oriented human resource management also contributes to the brand-oriented socialization of employees in all stages of their lifecycle (Piehler *et al.*, 2015). Depending on the socialization stage (Feldman, 1976; Van Maanen, 1976), organizations can apply specific brand-oriented human resource management practices. For example, in an anticipatory socialization stage (ie before potential employees join the organization), organizations can use *brand-oriented personnel recruitment and selection practices* (eg brand-oriented job advertisements, job interviews) to affect IBM outcomes such as brand understanding (Miles and Mangold, 2004, 2005; Aurand *et al.*, 2005; Ind, 2007; Mahnert and Torres, 2007; Punjaisri *et al.*, 2008; M'zungu *et al.*, 2010; Miles *et al.*, 2011; Piehler *et al.*, 2015). Burmann and Zeplin (2005) argue that the brand identity should be the basis for employer marketing and selection. Organizations should communicate the nature of the brand and its values to potential employees during the recruitment process (de Chernatony *et al.*, 2006; Ind, 2007). Then organizations can select employees whose personal identities are congruent with the brand's identity (Burmann and Zeplin, 2005; Ind, 2007), because it is hard to change personal identities but relatively easier to develop employees' technical and operational skills (Punjaisri and Wilson, 2007). Then in the encounter (ie entry) stage, organizations can apply *brand-oriented induction practices* (eg brand-oriented orientation, training, events) to encourage IBM outcomes such as brand understanding, brand identification, brand commitment, and BCB (Miles and Mangold, 2004; 2005; Aurand *et al.*, 2005; Burmann and Zeplin, 2005; de Chernatony *et al.*, 2006; Ind, 2007; Mahnert and Torres, 2007; Punjaisri and Wilson, 2007; Punjaisri *et al.*, 2008; 2009; M'zungu *et al.*, 2010; Miles *et al.*, 2011; Piehler *et al.*, 2015). Finally, in the metamorphosis stage, organizations can use *brand-oriented personnel development practices* (eg brand-oriented training, events, coaching, mentoring) and *reward and remuneration practices* (eg brand-oriented bonus systems, as well as brand-oriented evaluation, promotion, and dismissal criteria) to determine the IBM outcomes (Miles and Mangold, 2004, 2005; Aurand *et al.*, 2005; Burmann and Zeplin, 2005; de Chernatony *et al.*, 2006; Ind, 2007; Mahnert and Torres, 2007; Punjaisri and Wilson, 2007; Punjaisri *et al.*, 2008; M'zungu *et al.*, 2010; Miles *et al.*, 2011; Piehler *et al.*, 2015).

In their empirical work, Aurand *et al.* (2005) identify a strong relationship between human resources involvement in internal branding and the incorporation of the brand message into employees' daily work activities. With a qualitative study, de Chernatony *et al.* (2006) identify human resource activities such as selection, induction, and training as practices that make staff members aware of the brand's values, thus building brand understanding. Punjaisri and Wilson (2007, 2011) and Punjaisri *et al.* (2008, 2009) validate, in both qualitative and quantitative studies, how brand-oriented training and orientation positively affect brand identification, brand commitment, and brand-related employee behaviour. Additional empirical validation of the effect of brand-oriented human resource management on brand commitment comes from Burmann *et al.* (2009). Miles *et al.* (2011) show that recruitment and selection, training and development, performance assessment, and incentives that appear to reflect the organization's values increase employees' perceived knowledge of the organization's desired brand. Matanda and Ndubisi (2013) note that human resources' internal branding practices are antecedents of congruence between employees and their organization. In turn, the literature analysis by Saleem and Iglesias (2016) identifies brand-oriented human resource management as an important dimension of internal branding. Thus, brand-oriented human resource management represents an important managerial IBM practice that can influence the IBM outcomes of brand understanding, brand identification, brand commitment, and BCB.

Internal brand communication

Internal brand communication informs employees about the brand, engenders positive feelings, builds affective attachment, and influences employee behaviour. As part of internal communication, internal brand communication centres on brand-related information. According to Burmann and Zeplin (2005), internal brand communication consists of central, cascade, and lateral forms of communication. *Central communication* is the responsibility of a central communication department that distributes information through mass media (eg magazines, brand books, brochures, intranet) to create awareness and distribute general, updated information about the brand. *Cascade communication* instead comes from the top of the organization and moves through its hierarchy. This form of communication is more time consuming but also more convincing; employees receive information from a direct superior, so the information appears more relevant and credible than information from a central communication department.

Finally, *lateral communication* entails informal transmissions of information among employees, regardless of their position in the hierarchy or division. Although lateral communication is very powerful, with information coming from colleagues it is difficult to control or use deliberately for internal brand communication. Organizational storytelling is a promising approach to lateral communication though (Burmann and Zeplin, 2005; Ind, 2007).

Thomson *et al.* (1999) confirm that internal communication links to employees' intellectual buy-in, which relates to brand understanding, and to their emotional buy-in, which relates to brand commitment. Burmann and Zeplin (2005) also describe internal brand communication as a way to generate brand understanding and brand commitment. According to Burmann *et al.* (2009), internal brand communication is the strongest predictor of brand commitment; in a qualitative study, de Chernatony *et al.* (2006) also cite internal communication as a preferred tool for communicating brand values to employees, which affects brand understanding. Punjaisri and Wilson (2007, 2011) and Punjaisri *et al.* (2008, 2009) empirically affirm that internal communication positively affects brand identification, brand commitment, and brand-related employee behaviour; Punjaisri and Wilson (2007) also claim that internal communication affects employees' brand knowledge. In their empirical research, Baker *et al.* (2014) confirm the positive effect of brand knowledge dissemination on BCB through brand value congruence. Piehler *et al.* (2015) identify internal brand communication as an important managerial practice to build brand understanding, brand commitment, and BCB. Empirically, Porricelli *et al.* (2014) and du Preez and Bendixen (2015) confirm that internal brand communication affects brand commitment and BCB. In line with these findings, Saleem and Iglesias (2016) identify internal brand communication as an important internal branding dimension.

To influence the IBM outcomes of brand understanding, brand identification, brand commitment, and BCB, successful internal brand communication must exhibit the following features:

- segmentation (Mahnert and Torres, 2007);
- integrated communication (Burmann and Zeplin, 2005; Vallaster and de Chernatony, 2005; Punjaisri *et al.*, 2009);

- multidirectional communication (Vallaster and de Chernatony, 2005; Mahnert and Torres, 2007);

- interactive communication (Burmann and Zeplin, 2005; de Chernatony *et al.*, 2006; Ind, 2007; Piehler *et al.*, 2015);

- personal communication (Punjaisri *et al.*, 2008);

- quality of communication (Burmann and Zeplin, 2005; Baker *et al.*, 2014; Piehler *et al.*, 2015).

Mahnert and Torres (2007) propose segmenting employees when differences exist across employee groups, such as those defined by their tenure, hierarchical or departmental positions, geographical location, relevance to product and service production or delivery, demographic and psychographic criteria, or type and frequency of customer interactions. Employees divided by these features have different needs for information, which must be considered in relation to the development of internal brand communications. Internal brand communication also needs to follow an integrated communication approach, such that all communication tools are aligned in their message content, form, and timing. Organizations also should adopt multidirectional communication, by complementing top-down communication with bottom-up forms. The brand's identity and promise tend to be rather abstract, so interactive, two-way communication (eg brand workshops; Ind, 2007) can be more effective than one-way communication. In addition, personal communication, such as face-to-face conversations, tends to be superior to mass communication, which should be regarded as a backup medium. Finally, Burmann and Zeplin (2005) suggest that internal brand communication must be open, clear, specific, and relevant; Baker *et al.* (2014) identify timeliness, accuracy, and adequacy as key requirements. Similarly, Piehler *et al.* (2015) mention accuracy, timeliness, usefulness, completeness, and credibility of the information, which they subsume into a quality of communication dimension.

External brand communication

External brand communication, which involves the external communication of brand-related information, is also an antecedent of IBM outcomes. Although it primarily builds brand awareness and communicates the brand identity and brand promise to external stakeholders to build a positive brand image, internal stakeholders such as employees, are a 'second audience' (George and Berry, 1981, p. 52). In discussing internal effects of external communication, Acito and Ford (1980) investigate how advertising influences employees and argue that it can have as much effect on employees as it does on customers. They even suggest that advertising exerts stronger influences on employee attitudes and subsequent behaviour than internal communication, because advertising represents a public expression by management. George and Berry (1981) also see advertising as a tool to educate and motivate employees. By integrating marketing and organizational behaviour research, Wolfinbarger and Gilly (1991, 2005) and Gilly and Wolfinbarger (1992, 1998) develop a conceptual model of the impact of advertising on service employees' identification and commitment. Christensen (1997) and Cheney and Christensen (2001) combine organizational communications, marketing communications, and organizational identity research. The internal and external aspects of organizational communication are closely intertwined, leading Cheney and Christensen (2001, p. 258) to argue that 'communication that seems to be directed toward others may actually be auto-communicative, that is, directed primarily toward the self'. Organizations that express their identity through external communication leverage this self-enhancing dimension of external communication to instil pride among employees and even stimulate motivation and productivity (Christensen, 1997). In their quantitative study, Unzicker *et al.* (2000) identify a strong relationship between company–customer communication and employee perceptions of the firm.

In an IBM context, Miles and Mangold (2004, 2005) and Miles *et al.* (2011) describe employees as secondary recipients of external advertising and public relations messages and argue that both advertising and public relations can affect their perceived knowledge of the organization's desired brand. Burmann and Zeplin (2005) present external brand communication as part of central communication, influencing employees' brand commitment. Ind (2007) argues that external communication has the potential to affect employees' attitudes and behaviour. For de Chernatony *et al.* (2006), external communications, particularly advertising, are tools to influence employees' perceptions of brand values and thus to build brand understanding. With a foundation in services marketing research, Bowers and Martin (2007) suggest treating employees more like customers and using marketing communication to express the organization's values to these employees, which can reinforce its mission and purpose, motivate customer-contact employees, and heighten employees' sense of self-worth. In Henkel *et al.'s* (2007) behavioural branding model, mass media brand congruency functions as a predictor of employee performance. They argue that external communication shapes employees' thinking and behaviour, because it represents an implicit or explicit statement about the behaviours that employees are expected to perform. Continuing this stream of research, Wentzel *et al.* (2010) investigate when and to what extent service employees are motivated to live up to advertising that depicts how they are expected to perform. In their Consolidated Internal Branding Framework (CIBF), Mahnert and Torres (2007) suggest aligning internal and external messages to avoid confusion. Furthermore, M'zungu *et al.* (2010) recommend targeting employees in external brand communication, because it sets a standard for employees while also building their pride and commitment. Drawing on social identity and expectancy theories, Hughes (2013) uses survey and objective performance data to validate empirically the positive effect of employees' perception of brand advertising on their brand identification and brand effort. The quality of internal brand communication (adequacy, completeness, credibility, usefulness, clarity) also enhances the ability of perceived advertising quality to increase brand identification. According to du Preez and Bendixen (2015), external brand communication affects employees' brand commitment, and Piehler *et al.* (2015) establish external brand communication as an important antecedent of brand understanding, brand commitment, and BCB. In their literature analysis, Saleem and Iglesias (2016) thus include external brand communication as an important dimension of internal branding.

The requirements for successful external brand communication include:

- quantity and quality (Hughes, 2013);

- congruency of externally communicated product and service benefits with actual product and service benefits (Acito and Ford,

1980; George and Berry, 1981; Wolfinbarger and Gilly, 1991; 2005; Gilly and Wolfinbarger, 1998; Miles and Mangold, 2004; Piehler *et al.*, 2015);

- congruency of externally communicated culture with actual culture (Wolfinbarger and Gilly, 1991; 2005; Gilly and Wolfinbarger, 1998; Miles *et al.*, 2011; Piehler *et al.*, 2015);

- congruency of employees shown in external brand communication with actual employees (Wolfinbarger and Gilly, 1991; 2005; Gilly and Wolfinbarger, 1998; Bowers und Martin, 2007; Piehler *et al.*, 2015);

- congruency of external brand communication with internal brand communication (Acito and Ford, 1980; Mitchell, 2002; Miles and Mangold, 2004, 2005; Ind, 2007; Mahnert and Torres, 2007; Miles *et al.*, 2011; Piehler *et al.*, 2015).

First, both high quantity and quality of external brand communication can affect employee brand effort (Hughes, 2013). The effect of advertising quality on employee brand identification is even greater when accompanied by high-quality internal brand communication. Second, to ensure congruency in product and service benefits, external communication cannot make exaggerated brand promises that employees cannot fulfil. Gilly and Wolfinbarger (1998) reveal in their qualitative study that inaccurate advertising promises decrease identification and commitment, and then in a quantitative study, Wolfinbarger and Gilly (2005) confirm the negative effect of perceived exaggeration on ad-related attitudes, including identification. Henkel *et al.* (2007) similarly validate a positive effect of mass media brand congruency on employee performance. Third, congruency in culture means that the culture and values of the organization are portrayed accurately. Gilly and Wolfinbarger (1998) show that inaccurate portrayals and value incongruence lead to lower identification and commitment, and then Wolfinbarger and Gilly (2005) confirm that the perceived accuracy of an organizational portrayal positively affects ad-related attitudes, such as identification. Miles *et al.* (2011) empirically validate the notion that when advertising and public relations reflect the organization's values, they improve employees' perceived knowledge of the organization's desired brand. Fourth, employees need to be portrayed accurately, otherwise employee-related outcomes such as identification and commitment are hindered. Empirically, Wolfinbarger and Gilly (2005) confirm that the perceived accuracy of employees' portrayal has a positive effect on ad-related attitudes, including identification. To ensure this form of congruency, Henkel *et al.* (2007) and Bowers and Martin (2007) suggest using actual employees in external communications, because they are credible and offer advertising role models for other employees. Fifth, external brand communication requires congruency with internal brand communication (Ind, 2007), an aspect that relates to the integration of external and internal brand communication to avoid employee confusion and negative effects on IBM outcomes. Miles and Mangold (2004) argue that inconsistent internal and external communication disrupts employees' trust in and loyalty to the organization, as well as their willingness to deliver on the company's promises.

Conclusion

Successful brand management indirectly and directly depends on the delivery of the brand promise by employees. Therefore, employees represent a critical target group for brand management. By applying internal brand management, organizations can work to implement their brands cognitively, affectively, and behaviourally at the employee level. Brand management research offers several comprehensive models that include both IBM outcomes and managerial IBM practices; Figure 11.2 details the most important. Prior research specifies BCB (employee behaviours are consistent with the brand identity and brand promise, so they strengthen the brand) as a behavioural IBM outcome, brand identification (employees' feeling of belonging to the brand) and brand commitment (employees' emotional attachment to the brand) as affective IBM outcomes, and brand understanding (employees' comprehension of brand-related information) as a cognitive IBM outcome.

Regarding managerial IBM practices that can invoke these important employee-related IBM outcomes, organizations should rely

Figure 11.2 Internal brand management model

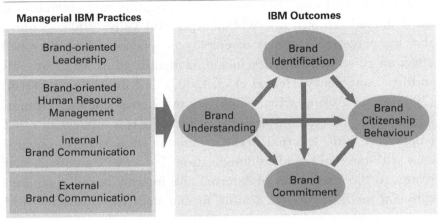

on brand-oriented leadership and brand-oriented human resource management as well as on internal and external brand communication. Concerning brand-oriented leadership, managers should use brand-oriented transactional, transformational and empowering forms of leadership. Specifically, managers should:

1 Specify behavioural standards for employees' role as brand representatives and reward employees when expectations are met.

2 Clarify what constitutes undesired behaviour as a brand representative and punish employees for not following the specified standards.

3 Act as a role model and live the brand.

4 Articulate the brand vision and arouse employees' involvement and pride in the brand.

5 Support employees to interpret the brand promise and its implications for their daily work.

6 Teach and coach employees to become brand representatives.

7 Share brand-related information and use employees' information and input in making brand-related decisions.

8 Delegate authority and encourage employees' self-directed decisions as brand representatives.

In the context of brand-oriented human resource management, managers should use brand-oriented personnel recruitment and selection, induction, personnel development, and reward and remuneration practices. Specifically, managers should:

1 Use the brand identity as a basis for employer marketing and selection in the anticipatory socialization stage through communication of the brand identity in job advertisements and job interviews and through consideration of congruency between personal identity and brand identity as selection criterion.

2 Apply brand-oriented orientation, training, and events in the encounter stage.

3 Employ brand-oriented training, events, coaching, and mentoring and install brand-oriented bonus systems, as well as brand-oriented evaluation, promotion, and dismissal criteria in the metamorphosis stage.

For internal brand communication, managers should use central communication in the form of mass media (eg magazines, brand books, brochures, intranet) to create awareness and distribute general, updated information about the brand. They should also apply cascade communication to better convince employees and communicate more credibly by passing brand-related information from the top of the organization through its hierarchy. Finally, managers should employ organizational storytelling to make use of lateral communication within the organization. When using these forms of internal brand communication, managers should:

1 Segment employees based on their tenure, hierarchical or departmental positions, geographical location, relevance to product and service production or delivery, demographic and psychographic criteria, or type and frequency of customer interactions.

2 Follow an integrated communication approach by aligning all communication tools in their message content, form, and timing.

3 Apply multidirectional communication by complementing top-down communication with bottom-up forms.

4 Employ interactive, two-way communication such as brand workshops and personal communication such as face-to-face conversations to successfully communicate usually rather abstract brand identities and promises to employees.

5 Ensure a high quality of communication through accuracy, timeliness, usefulness, completeness, and credibility of the information.

Finally, managers should consider employees as a second audience of external brand communication. To engender positive employee reactions, managers should ensure that:

1 External brand communication is characterized by a high quantity and quality.

2 External brand communication does not make exaggerated brand promises that employees cannot fulfil.

3 The culture and values of the organization are portrayed accurately in external brand communication.

4 Employees are portrayed accurately in external brand communication (eg by using actual employees).

5 External brand communication is aligned with internal brand communication to avoid employee confusion and negative effects on IBM outcomes.

References and further reading

Acito, F and Ford, J D (1980) How advertising affects employees, *Business Horizons*, **23** (1), pp. 53–59

Allen, N J and Meyer, J P (1990) The measurement and antecedents of affective, continuance and normative commitment to the organization, *Journal of Occupational Psychology*, **63** (1), pp. 1–18

Arnold, J A, Arad, S, Rhoades, J A and Drasgow, F (2000) The Empowering Leadership Questionnaire: The construction and validation of a new scale for measuring leader behaviors, *Journal of Organizational Behavior*, **21** (3), pp. 249–69

Ashforth, B E, Harrison, S H and Corley, K G (2008) Identification in organizations: An examination of four fundamental questions, *Journal of Management*, **34** (3), pp. 325–74

Aurand, T W, Gorchels, L and Bishop, T R (2005) Human resource management's role in internal branding: An opportunity for cross-functional brand message synergy, *Journal of Product & Brand Management*, 14 (3), pp. 163–69

Baker, T L, Rapp, A, Meyer, T and Mullins, R (2014) The role of brand communications on front line service employee beliefs, behaviors, and performance, *Journal of the Academy of Marketing Science*, **42** (6), pp. 642–57

Bandura, A (1977) *Social Learning Theory*, Englewood Cliffs: Prentice Hall

Bass, B M (1985) *Leadership and Performance Beyond Expectations*, New York: Free Press

Baumgarth, C and Schmidt, M (2010) How strong is the business-to-business brand in the workforce? An empirically-tested model of 'internal brand equity' in a business-to-business setting, *Industrial Marketing Management*, **39** (8), pp. 1250–60

Bergstrom, A, Blumenthal, D and Crothers, S (2002) Why internal branding matters: The case of Saab, *Corporate Reputation Review*, **5** (2/3), pp. 133–42

Bowers, M R and Martin, C L (2007) Trading places redux: Employees as customers, customers as employees, *Journal of Services Marketing*, **21** (2), pp. 88–98

Burmann, C and Zeplin, S (2005) Building brand commitment: A behavioural approach to internal brand management, *Journal of Brand Management*, **12** (4), pp. 279–300

Burmann, C, Zeplin, S and Riley, N-M.(2009) Key determinants of internal brand management success: An exploratory empirical analysis, *Journal of Brand Management*, **16** (4), pp. 264–84

Chang, A, Chiang, H H and Han, T S (2012) A multilevel investigation of relationships among brand-centered HRM, brand psychological ownership, brand citizenship behaviors, and customer satisfaction, *European Journal of Marketing*, **46** (5), pp. 626–62

Cheney, G and Christensen, L T (2001) Organizational identity: Linkages between internal and external communication, in F M Jablin and L L Putnam (eds.) *The New Handbook of Organizational Communication: Advances in theory, research, and methods*, Thousand Oaks: Sage Publications, pp. 231–69

Christensen, L T (1997) Marketing as auto-communication, *Consumption, Markets & Culture*, **1** (3), pp. 197–227

Cook, J and Wall, T (1980) New work attitude measures of trust, organizational commitment and personal need non-fulfilment, *Journal of Occupational Psychology*, **53** (1), pp. 39–52

De Chernatony, L, Cottam, S and Segal-Horn, S (2006) Communicating services brands' values internally and externally, *Service Industries Journal*, **26** (8), pp. 819–36

De Chernatony, L, Drury, S and Segal-Horn, S (2003) Building a services brand: Stages, people and orientations, *Service Industries Journal*, **23** (3), pp. 1–21

De Chernatony, L and Harris, F (2000) Developing corporate brands through considering internal and external stakeholders, *Corporate Reputation Review*, **3** (3), pp. 268–74

Du Preez, R and Bendixen, M T (2015) The impact of internal brand management on employee job satisfaction, brand commitment and intention to stay, *International Journal of Bank Marketing*, **33** (1), pp. 78–91

Dean, D, Arroyo-Gamez, R E, Punjaisri, K and Pich, C (2016) Internal brand co-creation: The experiential brand meaning cycle in higher education, *Journal of Business Research*, **69** (8), pp. 3041–48

Delgado-Ballester, E, Munuera-Alemán, J L and Yagüe-Guillén, M J (2003) Development and validation of a brand trust scale, *International Journal of Market Research*, **45** (1), pp. 35–53

Eatough, E M, Chang, C-H, Miloslavic, S A and Johnson, R E (2011) Relationships of role stressors with organizational citizenship behavior: A meta-analysis, *Journal of Applied Psychology*, **96** (3), pp. 619–32

Feldman, D C (1976) A contingency theory of socialization, *Administrative Science Quarterly*, **21** (3), pp. 433–52

Gautam, T, Van Dick, R and Wagner, U (2004) Organizational identification and organizational commitment: Distinct aspects of two related concepts, *Asian Journal of Social Psychology*, **7** (3), pp. 301–15

George, W R and Berry, L L (1981) Guidelines for the advertising of services, *Business Horizons*, **24** (4), pp. 52–56

Gilly, M C and Wolfinbarger, M F (1992) Does advertising affect your nurses? *Journal of Health Care Marketing*, **12** (3), pp. 24–31

Gilly, M C and Wolfinbarger, M F (1998) Advertising's internal audience, *Journal of Marketing*, **62** (1), pp. 69–88

Harris, F and de Chernatony, L (2001) Corporate branding and corporate brand performance, *European Journal of Marketing*, **35** (3/4), pp. 441–56

Henkel, S, Tomczak, T, Heitmann, M and Herrmann, A (2007) Managing brand consistent employee behaviour: Relevance and managerial control of behavioural branding, *Journal of Product & Brand Management*, **16** (5), pp. 310–20

Hughes, D E (2013) This ad's for you: The indirect effect of advertising perceptions on salesperson effort and performance, *Journal of the Academy of Marketing Science*, **41** (1), pp. 1–18

Ind, N (2001) *Living the Brand: How to transform every member of your organization into a brand champion*, London: Kogan Page

Ind, N (2003) Inside out: How employees build value, *Journal of Brand Management*, **10** (6), pp. 393–402

Ind, N (2007) *Living the brand: How to transform every member of your organization into a brand champion*, 3rd edn, London: Kogan Page

Johnson, M D, Morgeson, F P and Hekman, D R (2012) Cognitive and affective identification: Exploring the links between different forms of social identification and personality with work attitudes and behaviour, *Journal of Organizational Behavior*, **33** (8), pp. 1142–67

Kimpakorn, N and Tocquer, G (2009) Employees' commitment to brands in the service sector: Luxury hotel chains in Thailand, *Journal of Brand Management*, **16** (8), pp. 532–44

Kimpakorn, N and Tocquer, G (2010) Service brand equity and employee brand commitment, *Journal of Services Marketing*, **24** (5), pp. 378–88

King, C (2010) 'One size doesn't fit all': Tourism and hospitality employees' response to internal brand management, *International Journal of Contemporary Hospitality Management*, **22** (4), pp. 517–34

King, C and Grace, D (2010) Building and measuring employee-based brand equity, *European Journal of Marketing*, 44 (7/8), pp. 938–71

King, C and Grace, D (2012) Examining the antecedents of positive employee brand-related attitudes and behaviours, *European Journal of Marketing*, **46** (3), pp. 469–88

King, C, Grace, D and Funk, D C (2012) Employee brand equity: Scale development and validation, *Journal of Brand Management*, **19** (4), pp. 268–88

Konczak, L J, Stelly, D J and Trusty, M L (2000) Defining and measuring empowering leader behaviors: Development of an upward feedback instrument, *Educational & Psychological Measurement*, 60 (2), pp. 301–13

Löhndorf, B and Diamantopoulos, A (2014) Internal branding: Social identity and social exchange perspectives on turning employees into brand champions, *Journal of Service Research*, **17** (3), pp. 310–25

Mahnert, K F and Torres, A M (2007) The brand inside: The factors of failure and success in internal branding, *Irish Marketing Review*, **19** (1/2), pp. 54–63

Matanda, M J and Ndubisi, N O (2013) Internal marketing, internal branding, and organisational outcomes: The moderating role of perceived goal congruence, *Journal of Marketing Management*, **29** (9/10), pp. 1030–55

Merrilees, B and Frazer, L (2013) Internal branding: Franchisor leadership as a critical determinant, *Journal of Business Research*, **66** (2), pp. 158–64

Meyer, J P and Herscovitch, L (2001) Commitment in the workplace: Toward a general model, *Human Resource Management Review*, **11** (3), pp. 299–326

Meyer, J P, Stanley, D J, Herscovitch, L and Topolnytsky, L (2002) Affective, continuance, and normative commitment to the organization: A meta-analysis of antecedents, correlates, and consequences, *Journal of Vocational Behavior*, **61** (1), pp. 20–52

Miles, S J and Mangold, W G (2004) A conceptualization of the employee branding process, *Journal of Relationship Marketing*, **3** (2–3), pp. 65–87

Miles, S J and Mangold, W G (2005) Positioning Southwest Airlines through employee branding, *Business Horizons*, **48** (6), pp. 535–45

Miles, S J, Mangold, W G, Asree, S and Revell, J (2011) Assessing the employee brand: A census of one company, *Journal of Managerial Issues*, **23** (4), pp. 491–507

Mitchell, C. (2002). Selling the brand inside, *Harvard Business Review*, **80** (1), 99–105

Morhart, F M, Herzog, W and Tomczak, T (2009) Brand-specific leadership: Turning employees into brand champions, *Journal of Marketing*, **73** (5), pp. 122–42

Mosley, R W (2007) Customer experience, organisational culture and the employer brand, *Journal of Brand Management*, **15** (2), pp. 123–34

Mowday, R T, Steers, R M and Porter, L W (1979) The measurement of organizational commitment, *Journal of Vocational Behavior*, **14** (2), pp. 224–47

M'zungu, S D M, Merrilees, B and Miller, D (2010) Brand management to protect brand equity: A conceptual model, *Journal of Brand Management*, **17** (8), pp. 605–17

Nyadzayo, M W, Matanda, M J and Ewing, M T (2015) The impact of franchisor support, brand commitment, brand citizenship behavior, and franchisee experience on franchisee-perceived brand image, *Journal of Business Research*, **68** (9), pp. 1886–94

Nyadzayo, M W, Matanda, M J and Ewing, M T (2016) Franchisee-based brand equity: The role of brand relationship quality and brand citizenship behaviour, *Industrial Marketing Management*, **52**, pp. 163–74

O'Reilly, C A and Chatman, J (1986) Organizational commitment and psychological attachment: The effects of compliance, identification, and internalization on prosocial behaviour, *Journal of Applied Psychology*, **71** (3), pp. 492–99

Piehler, R, Hanisch, S and Burmann, C (2015) Internal branding: Relevance, management and challenges, *Marketing Review St. Gallen*, **32** (1), pp. 52–60

Piehler, R, King, C, Burmann, C and Xiong, L (2016) The importance of employee brand understanding, brand identification, and brand commitment in realizing brand citizenship behaviour, *European Journal of Marketing*, 50 (9/10), pp. 1575–1601

Podsakoff, P M, MacKenzie, S B and Bommer, W H (1996) Meta-analysis of the relationships between Kerr and Jermier's substitutes for leadership and employee job attitudes, role perceptions, and performance, *Journal of Applied Psychology*, 81 (4), pp. 380–99

Porricelli, M S, Yurova, Y, Abratt, R and Bendixen, M (2014) Antecedents of brand citizenship behavior in retailing, *Journal of Retailing and Consumer Services*, 21 (5), pp. 745–52

Punjaisri, K and Wilson, A (2007) The role of internal branding in the delivery of employee brand promise, *Journal of Brand Management*, 15 (1), pp. 57–70

Punjaisri, K and Wilson, A (2011) Internal branding process: Key mechanisms, outcomes and moderating factors, *European Journal of Marketing*, 45 (9/10), pp. 1521–37

Punjaisri, K, Evanschitzky, H and Wilson, A (2009) Internal branding: An enabler of employees' brand-supporting behaviours, *Journal of Service Management*, 20 (2), pp. 209–26

Punjaisri, K, Wilson, A and Evanschitzky, H (2008) Exploring the influences of internal branding on employees' brand promise delivery: Implications for strengthening customer-brand relationships, *Journal of Relationship Marketing*, 7 (4), pp. 407–24

Saleem, F Z and Iglesias, O (2016) Mapping the domain of the fragmented field of internal branding, *Journal of Product & Brand Management*, 25 (1), pp. 43–57

Shaari, H, Salleh, S M and Hussin, Z (2011) Exploring the dimension of internal brand citizenship behavior in Malaysia, *World Review of Business Research*, 1 (1), pp. 25–33

Sirianni, N J, Bitner, M J, Brown, S W and Mandel, N (2013) Branded service encounters: Strategically aligning employee behavior with the brand positioning, *Journal of Marketing*, 77 (6), pp. 108–23

Tajfel, H (1978) Social categorization, social identity and social comparison, in H. Tajfel (eds.) *Differentiation Between Social Groups*, London: Academic Press, pp. 61–76

Tajfel, H (1982) Social psychology of intergroup relations, *Annual Review of Psychology*, 33, pp. 1–39

Tajfel, H and Turner, J C (1986) The social identity theory of intergroup behaviour, in S Worchel and W G Austin (eds.) *Psychology of Intergroup Relations*, 2nd edn, Chicago: Nelson-Hall, pp. 7–24

Terglav, K, Konečnik Ruzzier, M and Kaše, R (2016) Internal branding process: Exploring the role of mediators in top management's
leadership-commitment relationship, *International Journal of
Hospitality Management*, 54, pp. 1–11

Thomson, K, de Chernatony, L, Arganbright, L and Khan, S (1999) The
buy-in benchmark: How staff understanding and commitment impact
brand and business performance, *Journal of Marketing Management*,
15 (8), pp. 819–35

Tuominen, S, Hirvonen, S, Reijonen, H and Laukkanen, T (2016)
The internal branding process and financial performance in service
companies: An examination of the required steps, *Journal of Brand
Management*, 23 (3), pp. 306–26

Unzicker, D, Clow, K E and Babakus, E (2000) The role of organizational communications on employee perceptions of a firm, *Journal of
Professional Services Marketing*, 21 (2), pp. 87–103

Vallaster, C and de Chernatony, L (2005) Internationalisation of services
brands: The role of leadership during the internal brand building
process, *Journal of Marketing Management*, 21 (1/2), pp. 181–203

Van Maanen, J (1976) Breaking in: Socialization to work, in R Dubin
(ed) *Handbook of Work, Organization, and Society*, Chicago: Rand
McNally, pp. 67–130

Wentzel, D, Henkel, S and Tomczak, T (2010) Can I live up to that ad?
Impact of implicit theories of ability on service employees' responses to
advertising, *Journal of Service Research*, 13 (2), pp. 137–52

Wolfinbarger, M F and Gilly, M C (1991) A conceptual model of the
impact of advertising on services, *Psychology and Marketing*, 8 (3),
pp. 215–37

Wolfinbarger, M F and Gilly, M C (2005) How firm advertising affects
employees' trust, organizational identification, and customer focus,
MSI-Reports, 05-002, pp. 20–39

Xiong, L, King, C and Piehler, R (2013) 'That's not my job': Exploring the
employee perspective to becoming brand ambassadors, *International
Journal of Hospitality Management*, 35 (December), pp. 348–59

INDEX